ENDURANCE
RUNNING THE RACE

AT A GLANCE

Serendipity House / P.O. Box 1012 / Littleton, CO 80160
TOLL FREE 1-800-525-9563 / www.serendipityhouse.com
© 1989, 1998 Serendipity House. All rights reserved.
SECOND EDITION
99 00 01 02 / **201S series•CHG** / 6 5 4 3

PROJECT ENGINEER:
Lyman Coleman

WRITING TEAM:
Richard Peace, Lyman Coleman, Matt Lockhart, Andrew Sloan, Cathy Tardif

PRODUCTION TEAM:
Christopher Werner, Sharon Penington, Erika Tiepel

COVER PHOTO:
© TSM / Pete Saloutos, 1998

CORE VALUES

Community: The purpose of this curriculum is to build community within the body of believers around Jesus Christ.

Group Process: To build community, the curriculum must be designed to take a group through a step-by-step process of sharing your story with one another.

Interactive Bible Study: To share your "story," the approach to Scripture in the curriculum needs to be open-ended and right brain—to "level the playing field" and encourage everyone to share.

Developmental Stages: To provide a healthy program in the life cycle of a group, the curriculum needs to offer courses on three levels of commitment: (1) Beginner Stage—low-level entry, high structure, to level the playing field; (2) Growth Stage—deeper Bible study, flexible structure, to encourage group accountability; (3) Discipleship Stage—in-depth Bible study, open structure, to move the group into high gear.

Target Audiences: To build community throughout the culture of the church, the curriculum needs to be flexible, adaptable and transferable into the structure of the average church.

ACKNOWLEDGMENTS

To Zondervan Bible Publishers
for permission to use
the NIV text,
The Holy Bible, New International Bible Society.
© 1973, 1978, 1984 by International Bible Society.
Used by permission of Zondervan Bible Publishers.

Questions & Answers

1. What stage in the life cycle of a small group is this course designed for?

Turn to the first page of the center section of this book. There you will see that this 201 course is designed for the second stage of a small group. In the Serendipity "Game Plan" for the multiplication of small groups, your group is in the Growth Stage.

GOALS

2. What are the goals of a 201 study course?

As shown on the second page of the center section (page M2), the focus in this second stage is equally balanced between Bible Study, Group Building, and Mission / Multiplication.

BIBLE STUDY

3. What is the approach to Bible Study in this course?

Take a look at page M3 of the center section. The objective in a 201 course is to discover what a book of the Bible, or a series of related Scripture passages, has to say to our lives today. We will study each passage seriously, but with a strong emphasis on practical application to daily living.

THREE-STAGE LIFE CYCLE OF A GROUP

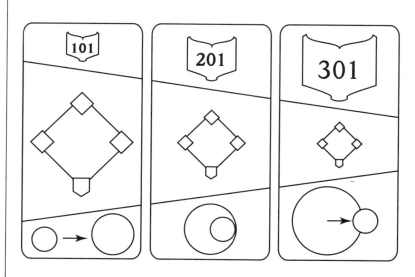

3

GROUP BUILDING

4. What is the meaning of the baseball diamond on pages M2 and M3 in relation to Group Building?

Every Serendipity course includes group building. First base is where we share our own stories; second base means affirming one another's stories; third base is sharing our personal needs; and home plate is deeply caring for each others' needs. In this 201 course we will continue "checking in" with each other and holding each other accountable to live the Christian life.

MISSION / MULTIPLICATION

5. What is the mission of a 201 group?

The mission of this 201 Covenant group is to discover the future leaders for starting a new group. (See graph on the previous page.) During this course, you will be challenged to identify three people and let this team use the Bible Study time to practice their skills. The center section will give you more details.

THE EMPTY CHAIR

6. How do we fill the "empty chair"?

First, pull up an empty chair during the group's prayer time and ask God to bring a new person to the group to fill it. Second, have everyone make a prospect list of people they could invite and keep this list on their refrigerator until they have contacted all those on their list.

AGENDA

7. What is the agenda for our group meetings?

A three-part agenda is found at the beginning of each session. Following the agenda and the recommended amount of time will keep your group on track and will keep the three goals of Bible Study, Group Building, and Mission / Multiplication in balance.

THE FEARLESS FOURSOME!

If you have more than seven people at a meeting, Serendipity recommends you divide into groups of 4 for the Bible Study. Count off around the group: "one, two, one, two, etc."—and have the "ones" move quickly to another room for the Bible Study. Ask one person to be the leader and follow the directions for the Bible Study time. After 30 minutes, the Group Leader will call "Time" and ask all groups to come together for the Caring Time.

ICE-BREAKERS

8. How do we decide what ice-breakers to use to begin the meetings?

Page M7 of the center section contains an index of ice-breakers in four categories: (1) those for getting acquainted in the first session or when a new person comes to a meeting; (2) those for the middle sessions to help you report in to your group; (3) those for the latter sessions to affirm each other and assign roles in preparation for starting a new group in the future; and (4) those for evaluating and reflecting in the final session.

GROUP COVENANT

9. What is a group covenant?

A group covenant is a "contract" that spells out your expectations and the ground rules for your group. It's very important that your group discuss these issues—preferably as part of the first session.

GROUND RULES

10. What are the ground rules for the group? (Check those you agree upon.)

❐ PRIORITY: While you are in the course, you give the group meetings priority.

❐ PARTICIPATION: Everyone participates and no one dominates.

❐ RESPECT: Everyone is given the right to their own opinion and all questions are encouraged and respected.

❐ CONFIDENTIALITY: Anything that is said in the meeting is never repeated outside the meeting.

❐ EMPTY CHAIR: The group stays open to new people at every meeting.

❐ SUPPORT: Permission is given to call upon each other in time of need—even in the middle of the night.

❐ ADVICE GIVING: Unsolicited advice is not allowed.

❐ MISSION: We agree to do everything in our power to start a new group as our mission (see center section).

Introduction to Philippians

Philippians is the letter of joy. Joy permeates its pages from start to finish. And yet this is not joy forged out of privilege and abundance. It is not the joy of people who have no problems to face. This is joy in the midst of hard situations. Paul is writing from prison. He faces the very real possibility of execution. The Philippian church is confronted with internal dissension and with false teachers who would seduce it away from the Gospel. Furthermore, both Paul and the Philippians live with the sense that the world might end any day. The second coming of Jesus was a living reality for them.

How can you be joyful in that kind of world? How can you urge joy when you are in prison? How can you experience joy when your fellowship is pressed from within and without? How can you be joyful when the world is about to end? The typical Christian today does not know how to answer these questions. To him or her, joy is what comes with prosperity and success. Joy is what happens when your church is growing and when its influence is spreading in the community. Joy is the anticipation of grandchildren who will build on the accomplishments of the family and do even better for themselves than you have done. Joy is the lack of pressure and hardship.

Since most of us are authentically puzzled by the emphasis in this epistle, it is therefore most important to listen carefully to what Paul has to say: It is not that we do not want joy. We do. We go to incredible lengths to find satisfaction (which is how we often define joy). It is just that we do not want joy in the midst of hardship. We want the hardship to go away. Yet, the hardship would not go away for either Paul or the Philippians. This was the reality in which they lived and out of which this letter, brimming with joy, was written.

The City of Philippi

Philippi was located in the Roman province of Macedonia (modern Greece), eight miles from the Mediterranean Sea in a fertile area known for its freshwater springs and gold mines.

Philippi was founded around 360 B.C. by Philip II, the king of Macedonia, so that he could mine its gold in order to finance his army. The city was named after him. Philip was the father of Alexander the Great. As a result of Rome's military conquests, Philippi came under Roman rule in 168 B.C. It rose to some importance then because of its strategic location on the *Via Egnatia,* the great road that linked Rome with the East. But its real prominence came later as the result of two battles. In 42 B.C., in the plains of Philippi, the Caesarean forces of Antony and Octavian defeated the Republican forces led by Brutus and Cassius, the assassins of Julius Caesar. A number of the soldiers from the victorious army were then settled there. A few years later, in 31 B.C., the two former allies fought each other at Actium. Octavian emerged victorious over the forces of Antony and the Egyptian Queen Cleopatra. Octavian later became the Emperor Caesar Augustus. After this second battle, yet more veterans were settled in Philippi, and it became a Roman colony. This meant that to live in Philippi was like living in Rome itself. One had all the rights and privileges accorded those in the capital. Its citizens were considered Roman citizens. Its governmental structure was modeled on that of Rome. The citizens were exempt from land tax and poll tax. At the time of Paul, the citizens of Philippi, who were mostly Romans (though there were some Greeks and a few Jews), were very proud of their city and its special tie to Rome.

The Founding of the Church

The church at Philippi was founded during Paul's second missionary journey. This had not been an easy journey for Paul. It began with the split-up of he and Barnabas and then after a time, Paul and his colleagues struggled to know where God wanted them to go. Acts 16:6–8 states:

Paul and his companions traveled throughout the region of Phrygia and Galatia, having been kept by the Holy Spirit from preaching the word in the province of Asia. When they came to the border of Mysia, they tried to enter Bithynia, but the Spirit of Jesus would not allow them to. So they passed by Mysia and went down to Troas.

It is in this context that Paul had his famous "night vision" in which a "man from Macedonia" beckoned him to "Come over ... and help us" (Acts 16:9). Paul did just that. He sailed almost immediately from Asia and after two days arrived at the Macedonian seaport of Neapolis. He was accompanied by Silas, Timothy, and now Luke (at this point in Acts, the report switches to the first person plural "we," indicating that Luke had joined the party).

Paul and his party did not remain at Neapolis, but pressed on to the city of Philippi to begin work. Paul's custom was to preach first in the local synagogue. But it seems that the Jewish population in Philippi was so small that there was no synagogue. Instead, a group of women met on the Sabbath by the banks of the river Gangites in order to recite prayers. Paul joined them and there he met Lydia, a successful merchant whose business was trading in the purple cloth for which her hometown of Thyatira was famous. She listened to Paul's message and was converted along with her whole household. They were the first European Christians. Lydia was not Jewish, but was a "God-fearer," that is, a Gentile who participated in Jewish worship without becoming a proselyte. Her house became the center of missionary activity in Philippi.

Paul soon ran into trouble in Philippi, however. It seems that he cast out a demon from a fortune-telling slave girl (though not without some hesitation on his part). She promptly lost her ability to predict the future. This outraged her owners, who saw that they stood to lose a great deal of money now that the girl was out from under the bondage of the demon. So they had Paul and Silas thrown in jail. That night, while the two of them were singing hymns and praying, an earthquake shook open the jail. The jailer saw the open door, and fearing that all his prisoners had fled, was about to commit suicide. But Paul stopped him and reported that all the prisoners were still there. With great emotion, the Philippian jailer inquired of Paul and Silas how he might be saved. Thus he and his household became Christians.

The next day, when the magistrates discovered that Paul and Silas were Roman citizens, they released them with some alarm. They did, however, "request" that they leave the city (one could not just throw a Roman citizen out of a Roman city). Thus Paul and Silas left Philippi, leaving behind them the first European church.

This church was always special to Paul, and he to it. Years later there was still a warm feeling of mutual care and concern between Paul and the Philippians, so much so that in his epistle Paul calls them his "joy and crown" (4:1).

It is quite possible that even though Paul and Silas had to leave Philippi, the church was not left without guidance. Luke may have stayed behind. The first "we" passage in Acts ends in Philippi (Acts 16:16) and the second "we" passage begins some years later in Philippi (Acts 20:5).

Origin of the Letter

When and where did Paul write Philippians? This is a question to which no certain answer can be given. However, one thing is clear. Paul was in prison when he wrote. Which prison he was in is not quite so clear. It is known that Paul was in at least four prisons. Chances are that he was also in other prisons on occasions not recorded in the New Testament. The four known imprisonments occurred in Philippi itself (Acts 16:19–40); in Jerusalem following the riot when it was rumored that Paul had brought Gentiles into the forbidden precincts of the temple (Acts 21:27–23:30); in Caesarea when he was awaiting a verdict on the charges leveled against him in Jerusalem (Acts 23:31–26:32); and in Rome where he was sent finally to be tried on the charges originating back in Jerusalem (Acts 28:30–31). Paul probably wrote this letter while he was in Rome under house arrest, awaiting trial, some time after A.D. 60.

The Occasion

Paul is in prison when Epaphroditus, an old friend from Philippi, arrives bearing a gift from the church. Unfortunately, Epaphroditus falls gravely ill. His home church hears about it and is deeply concerned. In due course he does recover, and Paul is anxious that he return home and relieve the fears of his friends and family. Epaphroditus' return to Philippi affords Paul the opportunity to send along a letter thanking them for their gift and for all that they mean to him. This also enables Paul to inform them that he hopes to send Timothy to see them soon, and that he himself will come when he is released from prison. He also warns them about the danger they face from certain troublemakers who seek to undermine both their doctrine and their morals, and to warn them about the internal danger they face due to their lack of unity.

This is the most personal of all Paul's epistles. He is writing to old friends and colleagues who have long supported his ministry. He does not have to assert his authority as an apostle (as he does in other letters). He is free to express his strong feelings toward them. There is an informality to this letter not found in Paul's other epistles.

One Letter or Two?

There is a problem with the epistle to the Philippians. It opens in a traditional way. Paul talks about his imprisonment and about how the Gospel is advancing. He makes an appeal for harmony among the members of the Philippian church. He tells them that he will be sending both Epaphroditus and Timothy to see them. And then in 3:1 he says, "Finally, my brothers ..." as if he is about to close the letter. But then he abruptly launches into a warning about dangerous men who will harm the church (3:2–21). This is followed by more exhortations (4:1–9) and by thanks for their gifts (4:10–20), after which he actually concludes his letter. So the question is raised: Is this a single unified letter or the composite of two (or more) letters?

Most commentators regard Philippians as a single letter, but it is instructive to note the two sections that could be separate letters. First, there is the warning about troublemakers that begins in 3:2 and goes to at least 4:1 (and possibly to 4:9). Then, second, there is Paul's note of thanks in 4:10–20. Still, these parts do not have to stand alone. The way in which they can be understood to be part of the whole letter will be made clear in the notes on each section.

THREE-PART AGENDA

ICE-BREAKER	BIBLE STUDY	CARING TIME
15 Minutes	30 Minutes	15–45 Minutes

> **LEADER:** *Be sure to read pages 3–5 in the front of this book, and go over the ground rules on page 5 with the group in this first session. See page M7 in the center section for a good ice-breaker. Have your group look at pages M1–M5 in the center section and fill out the team roster on page M5.*

TO BEGIN THE BIBLE STUDY TIME
(Choose 1 or 2)

1. When picking a card for a close friend, are you more likely to choose a funny or serious card?

2. What was the last letter (or e-mail) you sent? What was its purpose?

3. For whom or what do you thank God most often?

READ SCRIPTURE & DISCUSS
(If you don't have time for all the questions in this section, conclude the Bible Study [30 min.] by answering question #7.)

1. What one word best describes Paul's feelings for the Philippians?

2. What word would describe the feelings you have for your church?

3. What is unusual about Paul's positive attitude in this letter? (See the paragraphs on the Origin and Occasion of this letter on page 9.)

1 *Paul and Timothy, servants of Christ Jesus,*

To all the saints in Christ Jesus at Philippi, together with the overseers[a] *and deacons:*

²Grace and peace to you from God our Father and the Lord Jesus Christ.

Thanksgiving and Prayer

³I thank my God every time I remember you. ⁴In all my prayers for all of you, I always pray with joy ⁵because of your partnership in the gospel from the first day until now, ⁶being confident of this, that he who began a good work in you will carry it on to completion until the day of Christ Jesus.

⁷It is right for me to feel this way about all of you, since I have you in my heart; for whether I am in chains or defending and confirming the gospel, all of you share in God's grace with me. ⁸God can testify how I long for all of you with the affection of Christ Jesus.

⁹And this is my prayer: that your love may abound more and more in knowledge and depth of insight, ¹⁰so that you may be able to discern what is best and may be pure and blameless until the day of Christ, ¹¹filled with the fruit of righteousness that comes through Jesus Christ—to the glory and praise of God.

[a]1 Traditionally *bishops*

P.S. At the close, pass around your books and have everyone sign the Group Directory inside the front cover.

4. On a scale of 1 (easy) to 10 (hard), how hard is it for you to express your feelings like Paul did here?

5. How is God at work in a believer's life according to verses 6 and 9–11? How does this make you feel about uncertainties in your life?

6. Who was the "apostle Paul" in your spiritual life, the person who introduced you to Jesus Christ and cared about your spiritual growth?

7. Who is your spiritual cheerleader now?

CARING TIME

1. Has your group agreed on its group goals and covenant (see page 5 in the front of this book)?

2. Have you filled out your team roster (see page M5 in the center section)? Like any winning team, every position needs to be covered.

3. Verses 9–11 give us Paul's prayer for the Philippians. What is your prayer for this group?

Share prayer requests and close in prayer. Be sure to pray for "the empty chair" (p. 4).

Summary. In a typical Greek letter, following the salutation, a prayer was offered on behalf of the recipients. Paul follows this custom here, as he does in most of his letters. Specifically, he thanks God for the long partnership he has had with the Philippians. He expresses his gratitude (vv. 3–6) and his affection for them (vv. 7–8). Then he describes his prayer for them (vv. 9–11).

1:1 Timothy had long been a companion of Paul. Timothy was with Paul when he visited Philippi for the first time and so was well-known there. Paul may have dictated this letter to Timothy.

servants. Paul lived a life of willing submission to the Lord, a point he will stress as he calls upon the Christians to serve one another.

saints. This designation is the general New Testament word for Christians, who, because of their union with Christ, have been "set apart" to serve God.

overseers and deacons. The function of these individuals is not completely clear, except that they are leaders of some sort, quite possibly appointed by Paul.

1:2 *Grace and peace.* At this point in a Greek letter, the writer would say "rejoice." But here Paul wishes them "grace" which is a word that comes from the same Greek root as the secular greeting "rejoice." In a Hebrew letter, the writer would say "peace" (*shalom*). Paul links the two wishes together to form a distinctively Christian greeting.

1:3 *every time I remember you.* This is a difficult phrase to translate from the Greek. What it seems to mean is that during his times of prayer, Paul "was compelled by love to mention his Philippian friends. This means, then, that Paul gave thanks not whenever he happened to remember them, but that he regularly gave thanks for them and mentioned them to God at set times of prayer" (Hawthorne).

1:4 *prayers.* This is not the usual Greek word for prayer. (That word is found in verse 9.) This is a word that carries the idea of "need" or "lack," and so came to mean intercessory prayer. Paul is not just praying in general for the Philippians. He is praying that God will meet specific needs that he knows they have.

> *The "gospel" is the good news about what God has done in Christ Jesus to save men and women.*

with joy. "Joy" is a theme that pervades Philippians. This is the first of some 14 times that Paul will use the word in this epistle. He mentions "joy" more often in this short epistle than in any of his other letters. It is interesting that his first reference to joy is in connection with prayer.

1:5 *because of your partnership.* Paul is grateful to God for the Philippians, because they have always stood by him in the work of the Gospel. The Greek word rendered here as "partnership" is the familiar word *koinonia*, translated elsewhere as "fellowship." It means, literally, "having something in common." It is a favorite word of Paul's. Of the 19 times it appears in the New Testament, he uses it 13 times.

in the gospel. The Philippians were partners with Paul in spreading the Gospel. Specifically, they supported him financially in his ministry (2:25; 4:10–20). In addition, they worked with him to spread the Gospel (4:3); they prayed for him (1:19); and they contributed generously to the fund he raised in aid of the needy Christians in Jerusalem (2 Cor. 8:1–5). The word "gospel" is another favorite of Paul's. He uses it 60 of the 76 times it appears in the New Testament. It is used nine times in Philippians. The "gospel" is the good news about what God has done in Christ Jesus to save men and women.

1:6 *confident.* This is another of the underlying themes of Philippians—confidence. Paul makes it very clear what lies at the root of this confidence. It is not human accomplishment or ritual of any sort (3:3–4). This is confidence that springs out of faith in who God is and what he is doing. Here in this verse, he is confident that "he who began a good work in you will carry it on to completion ... ." Confidence, like joy, permeates this epistle.

good work. There is a difference of opinion as to the nature of this good work. Some would see this as the work of salvation begun in the lives of the

Philippians which will be consummated when the Lord returns. Others see this as a reference to the work of advancing the Gospel which will be carried on by the Philippians right up until the Second Coming. In other words, they will not cease in their financial support of Paul's ministry.

the day of Christ Jesus. This is the moment when Christ will return in glory and triumph to establish his kingdom on earth. This phrase is derived from the Old Testament phrase: "the day of the Lord" or "the day of Yahweh," which referred to the moment when God would vindicate himself and set right all injustice (see Amos 5:18–20).

1:7 feel. This is another favorite word of Paul's. It carries not only the idea of an attitude or an emotion (as in English), but also the concept of how one thinks about someone (or something) and what one plans to do because of these thoughts and feelings (which is not part of the English concept of "feeling"). "This word signifies a combination of intellectual and affective activity which touches head and heart, and leads to a positive course of action" (Martin).

since I have you in my heart. This phrase could equally well be translated, as in the NEB, "because you hold me in such affection." In this case, the way Paul "feels" about the Philippians is based on their affection for him. Perhaps the phrase is intended to be ambiguous and to be read both ways, since there was a mutuality of affection between Paul and the Philippians.

defending and confirming the gospel. These are legal terms. The reference is to Paul's defense before the Roman court, in which he hopes to be able not only to vindicate himself and the Gospel from false charges, but to proclaim the Gospel in life-changing power to those in the courtroom. (See Acts 26 for an example of how Paul did this when he stood in court before Agrippa and Festus.)

1:8 God can testify. In moments of deep feeling, Paul would sometimes invoke God to bear witness to the authenticity of these feelings (see also Rom. 1:9; 2 Cor. 11:11,31; 1 Thess. 2:5).

I long. Yet another word characteristic of Paul. He uses it seven of the nine times it is found in the New Testament. This is a strong word and expresses the depth of Paul's feelings for them, his desire to be with them, and the wish to minister to them.

all of you. Once again Paul emphasizes that his care is for every person in the church, not just for one group or for certain individuals. He loves the warring women (4:2–3) as much as Epaphroditus (who brought the gift to him). In first-century culture, a solemn oath such as he has just taken would be considered "proof" of the genuineness of his feelings (see Heb. 6:16).

1:9 this is my prayer. Paul's love for the Philippians leads him to prayer on their behalf. What he prays is that they will overflow with love. He prays that this love will increase (i.e., that it will go on developing) and that it will be regulated by knowledge and discernment.

knowledge and depth of insight. This growing love is to be focused by intellectual and moral insight. Both qualities are gifts from God. Both are nurtured by listening to wise teachers and learning from experience.

1:10 to discern what is best. The Philippians are confronted with competing ideologies as to what is true and how to live. They need "knowledge" and "insight" in order to choose and follow that which is of God and so results in "purity" and "blamelessness." The word translated "discern" is used to describe the process of testing coins so as to distinguish between those that are real and those that are counterfeit.

1:10–11 pure / blameless / fruit of righteousness. These three terms describe the kind of people this sort of focused love produces. These are people who are morally pure (i.e., their lives are transparent, free from stain), who give no offense or bring no harm to others, and who are authentically good people.

1:11 though Jesus Christ. The source of such goodness is the Lord.

2 Paul's Chains—Phil. 1:12–18a

THREE-PART AGENDA

ICE-BREAKER
15 Minutes

BIBLE STUDY
30 Minutes

CARING TIME
15–45 Minutes

> *LEADER: If there's a new person in your group in this session, start with an ice-breaker (see page M7 in the center section). Then begin the session with a word of prayer. If you have more than seven in your group, see the box about the "Fearless Foursome" on page 4. Count off around the group: "one, two, one, two, etc."—and have the "ones" move quickly to another room for the Bible Study.*

Bonhoeffer — Question
133   3

1 Peter 2:21
MARK 8:31
Bonhoeffer 96

TO BEGIN THE BIBLE STUDY TIME
(Choose 1 or 2)

1. Were you ever considered a troublemaker? Were you guilty or innocent?

2. When have you been stuck somewhere you would rather not have been?

3. When you have a bad day, what cheers you up?

READ SCRIPTURE & DISCUSS
(If you don't have time for all the questions in this section, conclude the Bible Study [30 min.] by answering question #7.)

1. Paul was in prison but joyful. What difficult circumstance are you dealing with? What's your attitude toward this situation?

2. What's the closest you've come to suffering for Christ? How does the possibility of being persecuted for your faith make you feel?

14

Paul's Chains Advance the Gospel

[12]Now I want you to know, brothers, that what has happened to me has really served to advance the gospel. [13]As a result, it has become clear throughout the whole palace guard[a] and to everyone else that I am in chains for Christ. [14]Because of my chains, most of the brothers in the Lord have been encouraged to speak the word of God more courageously and fearlessly.

[15]It is true that some preach Christ out of envy and rivalry, but others out of goodwill. [16]The latter do so in love, knowing that I am put here for the defense of the gospel. [17]The former preach Christ out of selfish ambition, not sincerely, supposing that they can stir up trouble for me while I am in chains.[b] [18]But what does it matter? The important thing is that in every way, whether from false motives or true, Christ is preached. And because of this I rejoice.

[a]13 Or *whole palace*   [b]16,17 Some late manuscripts have verses 16 and 17 in reverse order.

3. What has happened as a result of Paul's imprisonment (see notes on v. 13)?

4. What effect did Paul's situation have on most of his fellow believers (v. 14)?

5. What negative result did Paul's situation have on others in the church (vv. 15–17; see notes on v. 15)?

6. What does this passage say about what your attitude should be toward Christians whose motives you might question?

7. Where has God been able to use bad for good in your life?

P.S. Add new group members to the Group Directory inside the front cover.

CARING TIME
(Choose 1 or 2 of these questions before taking prayer requests and closing in prayer. Be sure to pray for the empty chair.)

1. As a way to "advance the gospel" (v. 12), who can you invite to join this group?

2. What challenges do you anticipate facing in the next week or two?

3. How can the group help you in prayer this week?

Summary. Paul began his letter in a traditional fashion with a salutation followed by thanksgiving and prayer. In verse 12 the letter proper begins and the first thing Paul does is to provide his friends with news about himself. He reports on what has happened as a result of his imprisonment. He points to three positive outcomes, all involving the advance of the Gospel: (1) The Gospel is being noticed by all sorts of people who might otherwise not have heard it (v. 13); (2) the Christians in Rome have become bolder in their own proclamation (v. 14); and (3) even though some of the preaching that is going on springs from wrong motives, still the Gospel is getting out (vv. 15–18).

1:12 *I want you to know.* This is a standard formula used in personal letters to indicate that the writer is now going to provide some information about his or her own circumstances. Paul assures them that good is coming out of his imprisonment. He does not at this point say much directly about the actual conditions of his imprisonment or the progress that has been made in terms of his forthcoming trial (perhaps it is dangerous for him to put such information in a letter), but he does assure them that all this has had a positive effect on the spread of the Gospel.

brothers. This is a generic term and means "brothers and sisters." By it Paul indicates the nature of his relationship with the Philippians. He and they are all part of one, big family—God's family. "Brothers" is a favorite term of Paul's. He uses it 133 times in his letters.

what has happened to me. This is literally "my affairs," and refers to the circumstances of his imprisonment about which he says little.

advance. A word used to describe an army that is marching forward despite obstacles. Paul's imprisonment could have had a negative effect on the spread of the Gospel. After all, here he was, the key evangelist, incarcerated and thus unable to get on with the preaching of the Gospel in the towns and the cities of the Roman world. Furthermore, his imprisonment could cast a shadow over his message. "What is he doing in jail if what he is preaching is legitimate?" potential converts might ask. But, in fact, the opposite has been true. Because of his imprisonment, the Gospel has spread all the more.

1:13 *palace guard.* These men were the elite soldiers in the Roman army, the bodyguards of the emperor. Because Paul had been sent to Rome for a hearing before the emperor, they were given the task of guarding him. Paul's guards changed every four hours or so, thus he got the chance to witness to a rotating coterie of soldiers from the key regiment in Rome. News of who he was and what he stood for apparently spread through the barracks and beyond into official circles. In 4:22, Paul will mention that some of those from Caesar's household had actually become Christians.

to everyone else. Paul's circumstances would also have become known to the officials preparing the case and to the others involved with the forthcoming trial. His trial may even have become the object of conversation in Rome.

in chains. Paul was not in a jail, but rather in a rented house where he was able to receive visitors, correspondence, and gifts (Acts 28:16,30; Phil. 4:18). He was, however, bound to a guard by a short length of chain that ran from his wrist to the guard's wrist. In such circumstances, it is not surprising that the guards got to know him and his Gospel.

for Christ. It had become clear to all involved that Paul was in prison not because he was a criminal who had been arrested for a crime he had committed, or because he had dangerous political views. He was in jail simply because he was a Christian. Thus, his arrest had cast no shadows on the name of Christ (see Acts 25:13–27; 26:30–32).

> *Paul's exclamation of joy is not how most people would sum up the experience of being in prison. But he has learned to see his circumstances in the light of God's plan; and so what matters is not how comfortable he is but whether the Gospel is thriving— and since it is, Paul can rejoice!*

1:14 Paul gives the second reason why his imprisonment had served to advance the Gospel. Because of his example, other Christians had become bolder in their own sharing of the Gospel, and so the message was being spread to even more people.

speak the word of God. This is the first of three terms Paul uses to describe the presentation of the Gospel. In verse 15 he says that some "preach Christ." The Greek word he uses there means "to do the work of a herald." In verses 17–18 he uses a third Greek word which means to "proclaim." The emphasis is not on how Christ is presented, but that he is presented!

more. Or "all the more." Paul does not mean that the Christians in Rome had not been preaching the Gospel prior to his imprisonment. It is just that now they have redoubled their efforts.

1:15 *some.* Although "most" (v. 14) of the brothers and sisters have been inspired by Paul's example to be bolder in proclaiming the Gospel, "some" have used his imprisonment as the opportunity to advance their own honor, prestige, or cause. However, Paul still considers these people to be "brothers." He may not like what they are doing, but he does not reject them as illegitimate members of God's family.

envy and rivalry. That which motivates these people is some sort of grudge or hostility directed against Paul. They did not like him and wanted to hurt him by their preaching. What lay behind this animosity is not clear. Perhaps they looked on Paul in disdain because he was in jail, seeing this as a judgment from God against him. ("If God were really on his side, then he would not have allowed him to remain in prison," they might have reasoned.) Or maybe they were jealous of Paul's role as an apostle and saw this as a golden opportunity to advance their own positions and prestige.

1:17 *selfish ambition.* Paul identifies still another motive on the part of his rivals. The Greek word translated "selfish ambition" has an interesting history. It originally meant a "day laborer." It came to mean someone who did "sordid work." It was used in the political realm to describe a person who had a "partisan spirit." Eventually, it came to refer to a relentless careerist who would do almost anything to promote his or her own advancement.

1:18 *false motives.* The three words by which Paul characterizes the motivation of his rivals—envy, rivalry, selfish ambition—are all words which he has used in other contexts to describe those actions and attitudes that are to be shunned by Christians. They are "vices that always adversely affect, even endanger, the life of the church (Rom. 1:29; 2 Cor. 12:20; Gal. 5:19–21; 1 Tim. 6:4)" (Hawthorne).

what does it matter ... I rejoice. There is about Paul a truly astonishing, magnanimous spirit which does not care for personal reputation (or who gets the credit) as long as the job gets done.

Christ is preached. The one fact that makes it possible for Paul to accept this situation—and in fact to find positive value in it—is that whatever else might be said about these wrongly motivated brothers and sisters, their message still centers on Christ.

because of this I rejoice. This is an unexpected conclusion to Paul's report on his imprisonment. One might have expected an appeal that they pray for him in his difficult circumstances or that they work to get him released. This exclamation of joy is not how most people would sum up the experience of being in prison. But Paul has learned to see his circumstances in the light of God's plan; and so what matters is not how comfortable he is but whether the Gospel is thriving—and since it is, Paul can rejoice!

3 Life or Death?—Phil. 1:18b–26

THREE-PART AGENDA

ICE-BREAKER
15 Minutes

BIBLE STUDY
30 Minutes

CARING TIME
15–45 Minutes

 LEADER: Remember to choose an appropriate ice-breaker if you have a new person at the meeting (see page M7 in the center section), and then begin with a prayer. If you have more than seven in your group, divide into groups of four for the Bible Study (see the box about the "Fearless Foursome" on page 4).

TO BEGIN THE BIBLE STUDY TIME
(Choose 1 or 2)

1. As a child, what was the first death you experienced: A pet? A grandparent? A family friend? How did it make you feel?

2. Are you brave or afraid when faced with: A spider? Snake? Mouse? Credit card bill?

3. Have you written a will? How do you feel about being kept alive on a mechanical life support system?

READ SCRIPTURE & DISCUSS
(If you don't have time for all the questions in this section, conclude the Bible Study [30 min.] by answering question #7.)

1. How do Paul's views about life and death contrast with typical views today?

2. Which option (life or death) does Paul personally desire (vv. 22–23)?

3. Why does Paul feel it is more necessary for him to do the opposite (vv. 24–26)?

Paul's Chains Advance the Gospel (continued)

*Yes, and I will continue to rejoice, ¹⁹for I know that through your prayers and the help given by the Spirit of Jesus Christ, what has happened to me will turn out for my deliverance.*ᵃ *²⁰I eagerly expect and hope that I will in no way be ashamed, but will have sufficient courage so that now as always Christ will be exalted in my body, whether by life or by death. ²¹For to me, to live is Christ and to die is gain. ²²If I am to go on living in the body, this will mean fruitful labor for me. Yet what shall I choose? I do not know! ²³I am torn between the two: I desire to depart and be with Christ, which is better by far; ²⁴but it is more necessary for you that I remain in the body. ²⁵Convinced of this, I know that I will remain, and I will continue with all of you for your progress and joy in the faith, ²⁶so that through my being with you again your joy in Christ Jesus will overflow on account of me.*

ᵃ 19 Or *salvation*

4. What is something you would like to accomplish before you die?

5. What difference has your personal faith in Jesus Christ made in your attitude toward death and dying?

6. Complete the following sentence: "For to me, to live is _____." Given your priorities and schedule this week, how would you honestly fill in the blank? What would change if you wrote "Christ"?

7. Share with the group a "progress and joy in the faith" (v. 25) report. How is your spiritual life going right now?

CARING TIME

(Choose 1 or 2 of these questions before taking prayer requests and closing in prayer. Be sure to pray for the empty chair.)

1. Who can you add to your "prospect list" to invite to this group?

2. Do you have a person for every position on the team roster (see page M5 in the center section)?

3. How can the group pray for you On your fears about life or death, or in your attitude right now?

Notes—Philippians 1:18b–26

Summary. Paul continues the report on his situation which he began in 1:12. (Notice how he continues to use the word "I" in this section.) In this unit, however, he shifts focus. In 1:12 he talked about the past (his arrest and imprisonment). In 1:13–18a he talked about the present (the advance of the Gospel). But here in 1:18b–26 Paul talks about the future (whether death or deliverance lies ahead for him). Paul displays a great deal of emotion as he contemplates what might lie ahead for him. His feelings go back and forth. One moment he is confident that he will be released. The next, he is worried that he might bring shame on himself or on Christ. He longs to be with Christ, but he also wants to go on living so that he will be a source of joy for the Philippians. On the other hand, it would be wonderful to lay down his burden and stand in the presence of the Lord that he has followed so long and served so faithfully. It is interesting to note that Paul is not at all reticent to express freely to his dear friends the full range of his emotions, including both his hopes and his fears.

> For Paul, his whole existence revolves around Christ. What he does, he does for Christ. He is inspired by Christ; he works for Christ; his sole focus in life is Christ. He is a man with a single, all-consuming passion.

1:18b *I will continue to rejoice.* The first reason that Paul rejoices is that the Gospel is being preached so widely (v. 18a). Here he gives his second reason for rejoicing: He expects to be delivered from prison.

1:19 *I know.* How he "knows" that all this will result in his deliverance is not certain. Probably what he is referring to is a deep inner conviction that God will make right this situation. His confidence is based on two factors: their prayers and the work of the Holy Spirit.

your prayers. Paul bases his confidence on two factors. This is the first: prayer. He knows that God hears and answers prayer. He knows that God acts in history because of prayer. And he knows that in the same way that he has been praying for the Philippians (1:4,9–11), they have been praying for him.

the help given by the Spirit. This is the second source of his confidence: the work of the Holy Spirit. The word used for "help" means, in a medical context, "the ligament which acts as a support" or in Greek drama it refers to the chorus which acts to support the whole play. The Holy Spirit will undergird and strengthen Paul "so that his courage will not fail nor his witness be impaired (v. 20)" (Martin).

1:20 *eagerly expect.* This is a rare word, used only here and in Romans 8:19. Paul may even have coined this word himself. It is "a picturesque word, denoting a state of keen anticipation of the future, the craving of the neck to catch a glimpse of what lies ahead" (Martin). Why was Paul so eager to be released from prison and so filled with the expectation that he would be? Certainly the reasons were not because he could not stand suffering, although he might wish to be freed from it (see 2 Cor. 4:17), or that he feared death (see vv. 21–23). Rather it was because release would demonstrate that he was innocent of any crime and especially prove that the Gospel he preached was not a subversive element in society aimed against the Roman government. Release would mean not only his vindication but that of the Gospel as well (Hawthorne).

hope that. Hawthorne disagrees with this translation. He feels that the word "that" is in the wrong place and that the phrase should read: "I know that I will not be ashamed ... ." If he is right, then in verses 19 and 20 Paul is saying that he knows two things (both introduced by "that")—that somehow he will be delivered and that he will not be ashamed.

ashamed. This is another rare word. In the New Testament, it is used only here and in 2 Corinthians 10:8. But unlike "eagerly expect," this word is used in other literature including the Old Testament. Depending upon where one puts the "that," this means (following the NIV rendering) that he is worried that he might disgrace either himself or the Gospel when he gets into court by not giving a proper defense. Or (following Hawthorne), it may mean that he knows that nothing in the trial can embarrass him or the Gospel.

courage. What Paul desires is the courage to speak boldly during his trial. This same word is used in Ephesians 6:19–20 where Paul expresses the identical desire. (Paul does not ask for courage to face his possible execution at the hands of the Romans. As he will point out in the next verse, death holds no terror for him.)

exalted. This word means, literally, to make something or someone large. When Paul uses this verb here he does not mean that his trial will succeed in making Christ greater, but rather that it will serve to make Christ, who is great, known to a larger audience.

by life or by death. By this phrase, Paul simply means that his single goal is to bring praise to Christ.

1:21–24 The phrase "by life or by death" seems to have caused Paul to reflect on these two realities. He is of two minds. Either option has value.

1:21 *to live is Christ.* For Paul, his whole existence revolves around Christ. What he does, he does for Christ. He is inspired by Christ; he works for Christ; his sole focus in life is Christ. He is a man with a single, all-consuming passion.

to die is gain. Precisely because Paul's sole ambition is to be "for Christ," his life has not been at all easy. In 2 Corinthians 11:23–29 he recounts a litany of struggles, beatings, imprisonment, shipwreck, hunger, etc. In Philippians he will mention some of these same hardships (e.g., 1:29–30; 3:10; 4:14). Thus, with a load this heavy, it is not a surprise that death would seem attractive. It is a way out from under it all. But, for Paul, there is more to it than merely escape. Death is the door into the presence of Christ. It is the path to reunion with the One with whom he is already in union. Death is not so much escape from hardship as it is entrance into joy.

1:22 Paul does not know which path is best. "To die is gain" but release from prison—which he anticipates—will give him the opportunity to do further missionary work. He may even be able to go to Spain as he had once planned (Rom. 15:24).

> *Death is the door into the presence of Christ. It is the path to reunion with the One with whom he is already in union. Death is not so much escape from hardship as it is entrance into joy.*

1:23 *to depart and be with Christ.* Death would be a gain for Paul since being with, in, and for Christ meant everything to him.

better by far. Literally, "much rather better." So strong is Paul's desire to be with Christ that he uses a triple adverb as an emphatic superlative to describe his preference.

1:24–25 There are two desires of equal force that press in on Paul: to be with Christ and to be with the Philippians. Since the Philippians clearly need him, he will stay. In fact, this is not something over which Paul has any personal control. The Romans will be the ones to release him or kill him. What Paul is doing in these verses is musing on theoretical possibilities. God is the one in ultimate control of his affairs. And since Paul is confident that he will be released from prison, the choice appears already to have been made for him. He will "remain in the body." This will have two results. The first is noted in this verse: He will help the Philippians to progress in the faith and to do so with joy.

1:26 The second result of Paul's release will be that his return to the Philippians will bring great joy to them.

4 Right Living —Philippians 1:27–2:4

THREE-PART AGENDA

ICE-BREAKER
15 Minutes

BIBLE STUDY
30 Minutes

CARING TIME
15–45 Minutes

> *LEADER: If there's a new person in this session, start with an ice-breaker from the center section (see page M7). Remember to stick closely to the three-part agenda and the time allowed for each segment. Is your group praying for the empty chair?*

TO BEGIN THE BIBLE STUDY TIME
(Choose 1 or 2)

1. What was the "unpardonable sin" in your family when you were growing up: Playing hooky? Cussing? Smoking? Playing poker? Missing curfew? Skipping church?

2. Who in your family taught you proper manners?

3. How has someone in this group been an encouragement to you?

READ SCRIPTURE & DISCUSS
(If you don't have time for all the questions in this section, conclude the Bible Study [30 min.] by answering question #8.)

1. Reading between the lines, what was wrong with the church in Philippi?

2. In addressing the Philippians' need for unity, what characteristics of a Christian community does Paul call them to strive for (2:2)?

[27]Whatever happens, conduct yourselves in a manner worthy of the gospel of Christ. Then, whether I come and see you or only hear about you in my absence, I will know that you stand firm in one spirit, contending as one man for the faith of the gospel [28]without being frightened in any way by those who oppose you. This is a sign to them that they will be destroyed, but that you will be saved—and that by God. [29]For it has been granted to you on behalf of Christ not only to believe on him, but also to suffer for him, [30]since you are going through the same struggle you saw I had, and now hear that I still have.

Imitating Christ's Humility

2 *If you have any encouragement from being united with Christ, if any comfort from his love, if any fellowship with the Spirit, if any tenderness and compassion, [2]then make my joy complete by being like-minded, having the same love, being one in spirit and purpose. [3]Do nothing out of selfish ambition or vain conceit, but in humility consider others better than yourselves. [4]Each of you should look not only to your own interests, but also to the interests of others.*

3. Does this mean that we have to agree on every issue (see note on "like-minded" for 2:2)? What kind of unity is important above all?

4. What are two things that will destroy Christian community (2:3)?

5. What are two things that will keep a Christian community from such problems (2:3–4)?

6. What is the message of this passage for your church?

7. Does someone oppose you, this group or your church? Do they frighten you? Should they? How should we handle opposition?

8. In what way do you find comfort in Christ's love?

CARING TIME
(Choose 1 or 2 of these questions before taking prayer requests and closing in prayer. Be sure to pray for the empty chair.)

1. What is the closest you have come to being in a fellowship that cared for one another like Paul describes here: Your buddies in the war? Your college sorority? A sports team? A recovery group? Other?

2. Who can you invite to this group next week?

3. Is there an area in your life you would like to ask this group to help hold you accountable for?

Notes—Philippians 1:27–2:4

Summary. Paul now shifts his focus from himself (and a report on his situation) to the Philippians (and advice on how to conduct themselves during the difficult times they are facing). The pronouns shift from "I" (in 1:12–26) to "you" in this new section (1:27–2:4). Paul began this letter by writing about his difficulties and in so doing allowed the Philippians to see how he dealt with pressure. Now he turns to their problems and offers insights that will enable them to cope creatively with the opposition they face. Paul first exhorts the Philippians to be unified (1:27–30). Then he tells them that unity is achieved by means of self-sacrificing humility (2:1–4).

1:27 *conduct yourselves*. Literally, "be a good citizen." The Greek concept of citizenship involved the idea of cooperation, interdependence, and mutuality, out of which each citizen attained his or her highest potential while assisting others to do the same.

> *"There apparently is a very real sense in which Christ needs people who are willing to take upon themselves the burden of his suffering in history that still remains to be borne."*

stand firm. This is a military term which conjures up images of a phalanx of Roman soldiers standing back to back, protecting each other while resisting the enemy. As long as everyone stood his place, such a formation was virtually impenetrable. The Philippians, too, are in battle and must adopt this same singleness of spirit and mind (unity) in the face of their enemies whose aim is to subvert the Gospel.

for the faith of the gospel. The goal is not victory on the battlefield, but the preservation of the Christian faith.

1:28 *without being frightened.* Yet another rare word, used in the Bible only this one time. Its original reference was to horses that were timid and which shied easily. The Philippians must not let their opponents spook them into an uncontrolled stampede.

those who oppose you. Paul does not identify their opponents. But in verse 30 he says "you are going through the same struggle you saw I had, and now hear that I still have." In both instances, Paul's opposition came from people who were opposed to his life and behavior as a Christian. In Philippi, this opposition came from secular merchants who were angry that he had freed a slave girl from bondage to an evil spirit. In Jerusalem, the opposition came from religious Jews who saw Paul's Christian faith as a threat to Judaism. The Philippians, too, are facing opposition of the same sort. A group of Christian Jews were advocating a return to the Law with all its rules and regulations.

1:29 *it has been granted.* It is assumed that Christians will suffer. But this is not something one has to put up with reluctantly because suffering for the sake of Christ is a gift of grace. Suffering is a privilege that has been granted to the Philippians.

on behalf of Christ. There are three senses in which this phrase can be interpreted. First, it could mean that they suffer "for Christ," i.e., because they are on his side, his enemies will harass them. Second, it could mean that they suffer "for the sake of Christ," i.e., because they love Christ they are willing to endure such difficulties. Or, third, it can mean (as it is correctly rendered in the NIV) that they suffer "instead of" Christ, or "in the place of" Christ. Their aim is to "complete what is lacking in Christ's afflictions for the sake of his body, that is, the church," as Paul says in Colossians 1:24 (RSV). "There apparently is a very real sense in which Christ needs people who are willing to take upon themselves the burden of his suffering in history that still remains to be borne" (Hawthorne).

1:30 *the same struggle.* Paul alludes to two incidents of persecution known by the Philippians: the one in Phillipi on his first visit there (Acts 16:16–40) and the other in Jerusalem that resulted in his present imprisonment (Acts 21:27–26:32). In each instance, Paul's struggle was with those who were opposed to his Christian beliefs and practices. In both cases his opponents stirred up the crowds against him and forced the Roman authorities to take him into custody. It is important to note that Paul was not being persecuted by Rome. His persecution originated with opponents of the Gospel. The Philippians are also facing the same sort of opponents.

2:1 By means of four clauses, Paul urges the Philippians to say "Yes" to his request that they live together in harmony. They have a strong incentive to be united to one another because of their experience of the encouragement, love, fellowship, mercy and compassion of God the Father, Son, and Holy Spirit.

If. In Greek, this construction assumes a positive response, e.g., "If you have any encouragement, as of course you do ..."

2:2 Paul continues to urge them to be united. In this verse, he uses four parallel clauses, each of which makes this point. He calls for them to "think the same way," to "have the same love," to be "one in soul," and finally, repeating himself, to "think the one thing." (These are literal renderings of the four Greek clauses.)

like-minded. This is literally, "think the same way." However, Paul is not just urging everyone to hold identical ideas and opinions. The word for "think" is far more comprehensive and involves not only one's mind, but one's feelings, attitudes and will. Paul is calling for a far deeper form of unity than simple doctrinal conformity.

one in spirit. In Greek, this is a single word which Paul probably made up since it is found nowhere else.

2:3–4 The road to unity is via the path of humble self-sacrifice. Paul has already demonstrated what he is urging here by means of his selfless attitude to those Christian brothers and sisters who preach Christ out of "selfish ambition" (see 1:17–18).

2:3 *selfish ambition.* This is the second time Paul has used this word (see note on 1:17 in Session 2). It means working to advance oneself without thought for others.

vain conceit. This is the only occurrence of this word in the New Testament. Translated literally, it means "vain glory" (*kenodoxia*) which is asserting oneself over God who alone is worthy of true glory (*doxa*). This is the sort of person who will arrogantly assert that he or she is right even though what that person holds is false. This is a person whose concern is for personal prestige.

humility. This was not a virtue that was valued by the Greek in the first century. They considered this to be the attitude of a slave, i.e., servility. In the Old Testament, however, this was understood to be the proper attitude to hold before God. What Paul means by humility is defined by the phrase that follows. Humility is "considering others better than yourself." Christians are to accord others the same dignity and respect that Christ has given to all people. Humility involves seeing others not on the basis of how clever, attractive, or pious they are, but through the eyes of Christ (who died for them).

2:4 *look not only to your own interests.* Preoccupation with personal interests, along with selfish ambition and vain conceit, make unity impossible. Individualism or partisanship work against community. Note that Paul says "look *not only* to your own interests." Personal interests are important (although not to the exclusion of everything else).

the interests of others. Instead, the Philippians should focus on the good points in others. "Rejoice in the honor paid to others rather than in that paid to yourself" (Bruce).

> *Humility is "considering others better than yourself." Christians are to accord others the same dignity and respect that Christ has given to all people. Humility involves seeing others not on the basis of how clever, attractive, or pious they are, but through the eyes of Christ (who died for them).*

THREE-PART AGENDA

ICE-BREAKER	BIBLE STUDY	CARING TIME
15 Minutes	30 Minutes	15–45 Minutes

 LEADER: Check page M7 in the center section for a good ice-breaker, particularly if you have a new person at this meeting. Is your group working well together—with everyone "fielding their position" as shown on the team roster on page M5?

TO BEGIN THE BIBLE STUDY TIME
(Choose 1 or 2)

1. Growing up, who was your role model—someone you looked up to? Why did you admire that person?

2. If you were to give yourself a grade for your attitude today, what would it be?

3. Who would you nominate from this group for the exceptional service award?

READ SCRIPTURE & DISCUSS
(If you don't have time for all the questions in this section, conclude the Bible Study [30 min.] by answering question #8.)

1. Where in your life could you use an "attitude adjustment"?

2. Verse 5 says, "Your attitude should be the same as that of Christ Jesus." What is his attitude? What is one way you can emulate the same attitude as Christ?

3. Why did Christ give up his position and power as the Son of God (vv. 6–7)?

Imitating Christ's Humility (continued)

⁵Your attitude should be the same as that of Christ Jesus:

⁶Who, being in very nature[a] *God,*
did not consider equality with God something
to be grasped,
⁷but made himself nothing,
taking the very nature[b] *of a servant,*
being made in human likeness.
⁸And being found in appearance as a man,
he humbled himself
and became obedient to death—
even death on a cross!
⁹Therefore God exalted him to the highest place
and gave him the name that is above every
name,
¹⁰that at the name of Jesus every knee should bow,
in heaven and on earth and under the earth,
¹¹and every tongue confess that Jesus Christ is
Lord,
to the glory of God the Father.

[a]6 Or *in the form of*   [b]7 Or *the form*

4. What was the ultimate decision Jesus made in giving us an example of humility (v. 8)?

5. Although the stress is on Jesus' humility, what else stands out about him in this passage?

6. How does this passage challenge society's definition of success? What is your definition of success?

7. What is one specific way you can imitate Christ's humility this coming week?

8. What is something this group can do this week to serve someone else?

CARING TIME

(Choose 1 or 2 of these questions before taking prayer requests and closing in prayer. Be sure to pray for the empty chair.)

1. How are you doing on inviting people from your "prospect list" to this group?

2. Are all the players on the team roster fulfilling all of the assignments of their position? (Look at the roster again on page M5 of the center section.)

3. How can this group pray for you this week?

Notes—Philippians 2:5–11

Summary. From a theological point of view, this is the most important section in Philippians. Here Paul provides an amazing glimpse into the nature of Jesus Christ. Through Paul's eyes we see Jesus, the divine Savior who comes to his people in humility not in power; we see the Lord of the Universe before whom all bow choosing to die for his subjects; we see one who is in nature God, voluntarily descending to the depths (and becoming a servant) before he is lifted up to the heights (and assumes his kingship). This is a breathtaking glimpse that is made all the more astonishing because no one ever imagined that God would work his will in such a way. Who would have thought that God would act via weakness not via power?

When Paul wrote these verses his main intention was not to make a theological point. Rather, his aim was to illustrate what self-sacrificing humility was all about. This is why he turns to the example of Jesus—he is the best illustration of a humble person that Paul knows. To demonstrate the humility of Christ, Paul quotes from an ancient Christian hymn about Jesus. Perhaps he composed the hymn himself. In quoting this hymn, Paul provides a fascinating glimpse into how the early Christians viewed Jesus. He also gives us one of the few existing examples of early church hymnology.

2:5 This is the transition verse between the exhortation of 2:1–4 and the illustration of 2:6–11. In it Paul states that the model for the sort of self-sacrificing humility he has been urging is found in Jesus.

2:6–11 There is little agreement between scholars as to how this hymn breaks into verses or how it is to be phrased. However, one thing is clear. The hymn has two equal parts. Part one (vv. 6–8) focuses on the self-humiliation of Jesus. Part two (vv. 9–11) focuses on God's exaltation of Jesus. In part one, Jesus is the subject of the two main verbs, while in part two, God is the subject of the two main verbs.

2:6 being. This is not the normal Greek word for "being." "It describes that which a man is in his very essence, that which cannot be changed" (Barclay). This word also carries the idea of pre-existence. By using it, Paul is saying that Jesus always existed in the form of God.

very nature. The Greek word here is *morphe* (used twice by Paul in this hymn). He says that Jesus was "in very nature God," and that he then took upon himself "the very nature of a servant." This is a key word in understanding the nature of Christ. Barclay defines *morphe* as "the essential form of something which never alters," in contrast to the word *schema* (used by Paul in v. 7), which denotes outward and changeable forms. In other words, Jesus possessed the essential nature of God. Why doesn't he say this more directly? In the same way that a Jew could not bring himself to pronounce the name of God, a strict monotheist like Paul cannot quite bring himself to say bluntly: "Jesus is God," though he winds up saying this very thing.

> *It is significant that the one before whom all will bow is Jesus, the man from Nazareth. The cosmic Lord is none other than the person who walked the roads of Palestine and talked to the people of Israel. He had a hometown, a family, a trade, and disciples. The one before whom Christians will stand at the Last Judgment is not an anonymous Life Force, but the man of Galilee who has a familiar face.*

to be grasped. This is another rare word, used only at this point in the New Testament. It refers to the fact that Jesus did not have to "snatch" equality with God. Equality was not something he needed to acquire. It was his already, and thus he could give it away. Giving, not grasping, is what Jesus did.

2:7 made himself nothing. Literally, "to empty," or "to pour out until the container is empty."

taking the very nature of a servant. Jesus gave up Godhood and took on slavehood. From being the ultimate master, he became the lowest servant. He left ruling for serving. *Morphe* is used here again, indicating that Jesus adopted the essential nature of a slave. He did not "play act" being a slave for a time. The use of the word "slave" here "empha-

Game Plan

Leadership Training Supplement

YOU ARE
HERE

BIRTH	GROWTH	RELEASE

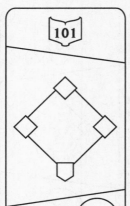
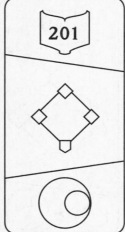
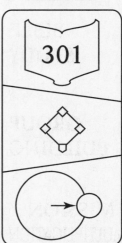

What is the game plan for your group in the 201 stage?

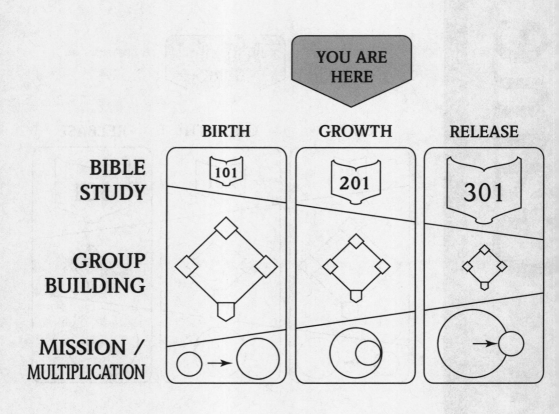

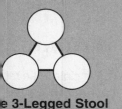

e 3-Legged Stool

The three essentials in a healthy small group are Bible Study, Group Building and Mission / Multiplication. You need all three to stay balanced—like a 3-legged stool.
- To focus only on Bible Study will lead to scholasticism.
- To focus only on Group Building will lead to narcissism.
- To focus only on Mission will lead to burnout.

You need a game plan for the life cycle of the group where all of these elements are present in a purpose-driven strategy.

Bible Study

To dig into Scripture as a group.

Group Bible Study is quite different from individual Bible Study. The guided discussion questions are open-ended. And for those with little Bible background, there are reference notes to bring this person up to speed.

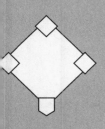

Group Building

To transform your group into a mission-driven team.

The nine basic needs of a group will be assigned to nine different people. Everyone has a job to fill, and when everyone is doing their job the group will grow spiritually and numerically. When new people enter the group, there is a selection of ICE-BREAKERS to start off the meeting and let the new people get acquainted.

Mission / Multiplication

To identify the Apprentice / Leader for birthing a new group.

In this stage, you will start dreaming about the possibility of starting a new group down the road. The questions at the close of each session will lead you carefully through the dreaming process—to help you discover an Apprentice / Leader who will eventually be the leader of a new group. This is an exciting challenge!

Bible Study

What is unique about Serendipity Group Bible Study?

Bible Study for groups is based on six principles. Principle 1: Level the playing field so that everyone can share—those who know the Bible and those who do not know the Bible. Principle 2: Share your spiritual story and let the people in your group get to know you. Principle 3: Ask open-ended questions that have no right or wrong answers. Principle 4: Keep a tight agenda. Principle 5: Subdivide into smaller groups so that everyone can participate. Principle 6: Affirm One Another—"Thanks for sharing."

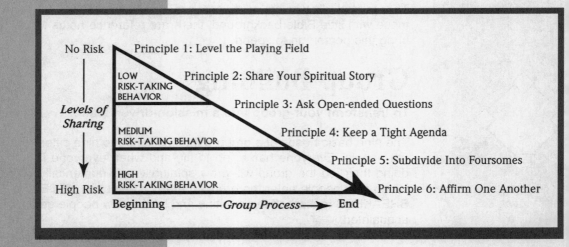

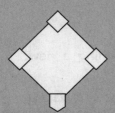

Group Building

What are the jobs that are needed on your team roster?

In the first or second session of this course, you need to fill out the roster on the next page. Then check every few weeks to see that everyone is "playing their position." If you do not have nine people in your group, you can double up on jobs until new people join your group and are assigned a job.

Your Small Group Team Roster

Mission Leader
(Left Field)
Keeps group focused on the mission to invite new people and eventually give birth to a new group. This person needs to be passionate and have a long-term perspective.

Host
(Center Field)
Environmental engineer in charge of meeting location. Always on the lookout for moving to a new meeting location where new people will feel the "home field advantage."

Social Leader
(Right Field)
Designates who is going to bring refreshments. Plans a party every month or so where new people are invited to visit and children are welcome.

Caretaker
(Shortstop)
Takes new members under their wing. Makes sure they get acquainted. Always has an extra book, name tags and a list of group members and phone numbers.

Bible Study Leader
(Second Base)
Takes over in the Bible Study time (30 minutes). Follows the agenda. Keeps the group moving. This person must be very time-conscious.

Group Leader
(Pitcher)
Puts ball in play. Team encourager. Motivator. Sees to it that everyone is involved in the team effort.

Caring Time Leader
(Third Base)
Takes over in the Caring Time. Records prayer requests and follows up on any prayer needs during the week. This person is the "heart" of the group.

Worship Leader
(First Base)
Starts the meeting with singing and prayer. If a new person comes, shifts immediately to an ice-breaker to get acquainted, before the opening prayer.

Apprentice / Leader
(Catcher)
The other half of the battery. Observes the infield. Calls "time" to discuss strategy and regroup. Stays focused.

Leadership Training

Mission / Multiplication

Where are you in the 3-stage life cycle of your mission?

You can't sit on a one-legged stool—or even a two-legged stool. It takes all three. The same is true of a small group; you need all three legs. A Bible Study and Care Group will eventually fall if it does not have a mission.

The mission goal is to eventually give birth to a new group. In this 201 course, the goals are: 1) to keep inviting new people to join your group and 2) to discover the Apprentice / Leader and leadership core for starting a new group down the road.

When a new person comes to the group, start off the meeting with one of the ice-breakers on the following pages. These ice-breakers are designed to be fun and easy to share, but they have a very important purpose—that is, to let the new person get acquainted with the group and share their spiritual story with the group, and hear the spiritual stories of those in the group.

YOU ARE
HERE

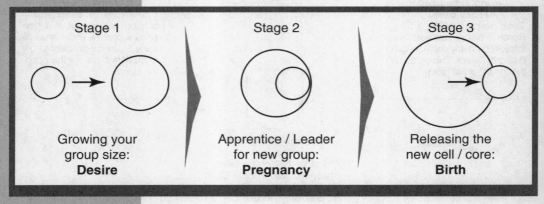

Stage 1	Stage 2	Stage 3
Growing your group size: **Desire**	Apprentice / Leader for new group: **Pregnancy**	Releasing the new cell / core: **Birth**

M6

Group Building

Ice-Breakers

Session 1
or when
a new person
comes to a
meeting

Get Acquainted / New People

ddle Sessions

To Report In to Your Group

atter Sessions

To Affirm and Assign Roles

Last Session

To Evaluate and Say Good-bye

I Am Somebody Who ...

Rotate around the group, one person reading the first item, the next person reading the second item, etc. Before answering, let everyone in the group try to GUESS what the answer would be: "Yes" ... "No" ... or "Maybe." After everyone has guessed, explain the answer. Anyone who guessed right gets $10. When every item on the list has been read, the person with the most "money" WINS.

I AM SOMEBODY WHO ...

Y N M
- ❏ ❏ ❏ would go on a blind date
- ❏ ❏ ❏ sings in the shower
- ❏ ❏ ❏ listens to music full blast
- ❏ ❏ ❏ likes to dance
- ❏ ❏ ❏ cries at movies
- ❏ ❏ ❏ stops to smell the flowers
- ❏ ❏ ❏ daydreams a lot
- ❏ ❏ ❏ likes to play practical jokes
- ❏ ❏ ❏ makes a "to do" list
- ❏ ❏ ❏ loves liver
- ❏ ❏ ❏ won't use a portable toilet
- ❏ ❏ ❏ likes thunderstorms
- ❏ ❏ ❏ enjoys romance novels
- ❏ ❏ ❏ loves crossword puzzles
- ❏ ❏ ❏ hates flying
- ❏ ❏ ❏ fixes my own car

Y N M
- ❏ ❏ ❏ would enjoy skydiving
- ❏ ❏ ❏ has a black belt in karate
- ❏ ❏ ❏ watches soap operas
- ❏ ❏ ❏ is afraid of the dark
- ❏ ❏ ❏ goes to bed early
- ❏ ❏ ❏ plays the guitar
- ❏ ❏ ❏ talks to plants
- ❏ ❏ ❏ will ask a stranger for directions
- ❏ ❏ ❏ sleeps until the last second
- ❏ ❏ ❏ likes to travel alone
- ❏ ❏ ❏ reads the financial page
- ❏ ❏ ❏ saves for a rainy day
- ❏ ❏ ❏ lies about my age
- ❏ ❏ ❏ yells at the umpire
- ❏ ❏ ❏ closes my eyes during scary movies

Press Conference

This is a great activity for a new group or when new people are joining an established group. Interview one person with these questions.

1. What is your nickname and how did you get it?

2. Where did you grow up? Where was the "watering hole" in your hometown—where kids got together?

3. What did you do for kicks then? What about now?

4. What was the turning point in your spiritual life?

5. What prompted you to come to this group?

6. What do you want to get out of this group?

Down Memory Lane

Celebrate the childhood memories of the way you were. Choose one or more of the topics listed below and answer the question related to it. If time allows, do another round.

HOME SWEET HOME–What do you remember about your childhood home?

TELEVISION—What was your favorite TV program or radio show?

OLD SCHOOLHOUSE—What were your best and worst subjects in school?

LIBRARY—What did you like to read (and where)?

TELEPHONE—How much time did you spend on the phone each day?

MOVIES—Who was your favorite movie star?

CASH FLOW—What did you do for spending money?

SPORTS—What was your favorite sport or team?

GRANDPA'S HOUSE—Where did your grandparents live? When did you visit them?

POLICE—Did you ever get in trouble with the law?

WEEKENDS—What was the thing to do on Saturday night?

Wallet Scavenger Hunt

With your wallet or purse, use the set of questions below. You get two minutes in silence to go through your possessions and find these items. Then break the silence and "show-and-tell" what you have chosen. For instance, "The thing I have had for the longest time is ... this picture of me when I was a baby."

1. The thing I have had for the LONGEST TIME in my wallet is ...

2. The thing that has SENTIMENTAL VALUE is ...

3. The thing that reminds me of a FUN TIME is ...

4. The most REVEALING thing about me in my wallet is ...

The Grand Total

This is a fun ice-breaker that has additional uses. You can use this ice-breaker to divide your group into two subgroups (odds and evens). You can also calculate who has the highest and lowest totals if you need a fun way to select someone to do a particular task, such as bring refreshments or be first to tell their story.

Fill each box with the correct number and then total your score. When everyone is finished, go around the group and explain how you got your total.

☐ X	☐ =	☐
Number of hours you sleep	Number of miles you walk daily	Subtotal

☐ −	☐ =	☐
Number of speeding tickets you've received	Number of times sent to principal's office	Subtotal

☐ ÷	☐ =	☐
Number of books you read this year for fun	Number of hours spent watching TV daily	Subtotal

☐ +	☐ =	☐
Number of push-ups you can do	Number of pounds you lost this year	Subtotal

☐

GRAND TOTAL

Find Yourself in the Picture

In this drawing, which child do you identify with—or which one best portrays you right now? Share with your group which child you would choose and why. You can also use this as an affirmation exercise, by assigning each person in your group to a child in the picture.

Four Facts, One Lie

Everyone in the group should answer the following five questions. One of the five answers should be a lie! The rest of the group members can guess which of your answers is a lie.

1. At age 7, my favorite TV show was ...

2. At age 9, my hero was ...

3. At age 11, I wanted to be a ...

4. At age 13, my favorite music was ...

5. Right now, my favorite pastime is ...

Old-Fashioned Auction

Just like an old-fashioned auction, conduct an out loud auction in your group—starting each item at $50. Everybody starts out with $1,000. Select an auctioneer. This person can also get in on the bidding. Remember, start the bidding on each item at $50. Then, write the winning bid in the left column and the winner's name in the right column. Remember, you only have $1,000 to spend for the whole game. AUCTIONEER: Start off by asking, "Who will give me $50 for a 1965 red MG convertible?" ... and keep going until you have a winner. Keep this auction to 10 minutes.

WINNING BID		WINNER
$_____	1965 red MG convertible in perfect condition	_____
$_____	Winter vacation in Hawaii for two	_____
$_____	Two Super Bowl tickets on the 50-yard line	_____
$_____	One year of no hassles with my kids / parents	_____
$_____	Holy Land tour hosted by my favorite Christian leader	_____
$_____	Season pass to ski resort of my choice	_____
$_____	Two months off to do anything I want, with pay	_____
$_____	Home theater with surround sound	_____
$_____	Breakfast in bed for one year	_____
$_____	Two front-row tickets at the concert of my choice	_____
$_____	Two-week Caribbean cruise with my spouse in honeymoon suite	_____
$_____	Shopping spree at Saks Fifth Avenue	_____
$_____	Six months of maid service	_____
$_____	All-expense-paid family vacation to Disney World	_____

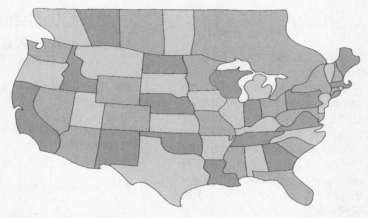

Places in My Life

On the map above, put six dots to indicate these significant places in your journey. Then go around and have each person explain the dots:

- the place where I was born
- the place where I spent most of my life
- the place where I first fell in love
- the place where I went or would like to go on a honeymoon
- the place where God first became real to me
- the place where I would like to retire

The Four Quaker Questions

This is an old Quaker activity which Serendipity has adapted over the years. Go around the group and share your answers to the questions, everyone answering #1. Then, everyone answers #2, etc. This ice-breaker has been known to take between 30 and 60 minutes for some groups.

1. Where were you living between the ages of 7 and 12, and what were the winters like then?

2. How was your home heated during that time?

3. What was the center of warmth in your life when you were a child? (It could be a place in the house, a time of year, a person, etc.)

4. When did God become a "warm" person to you ... and how did it happen?

KWIZ Show

Like a TV quiz show, someone from the group picks a category and reads the four questions—pausing to let the others in the group guess before revealing the answer. When the first person is finished, everyone adds up the money they won by guessing right. Go around the group and have each person take a category. The person with the most money at the end wins. To begin, ask one person to choose a CATEGORY and read out loud the $1 question. Before answering, let everyone try to GUESS the answer. When everyone has guessed, the person answers the question, and anyone who guessed right puts $1 in the margin, etc. until the first person has read all four questions in the CATEGORY.

Clothes

For $1: I'm more likely to shop at:
❐ Sears   ❐ Saks Fifth Avenue

For $2: I feel more comfortable wearing:
❐ formal clothes
❐ casual clothes
❐ sport clothes
❐ grubbies

For $3: In buying clothes, I look for:
❐ fashion / style
❐ price
❐ name brand
❐ quality

For $4: In buying clothes, I usually:
❐ shop all day for a bargain
❐ go to one store, but try on everything
❐ buy the first thing I try on
❐ buy without trying it on

Tastes

For $1: In music, I am closer to:
❐ Bach   ❐ Beatles

For $2: In furniture, I prefer:
❐ Early American
❐ French Provincial
❐ Scandinavian—contemporary
❐ Hodgepodge—little of everything

For $3: My choice of reading material is:
❐ science fiction   ❐ sports
❐ mystery   ❐ romance

For $4: If I had $1,000 to splurge, I would buy:
❐ one original painting
❐ two numbered prints
❐ three reproductions and an easy chair
❐ four cheap imitations, easy chair and color TV

Travel

For $1: For travel, I prefer:
❐ excitement   ❐ enrichment

For $2: On a vacation, my lifestyle is:
❐ go-go all the time
❐ slow and easy
❐ party every night and sleep in

For $3: In packing for a trip, I include:
❐ toothbrush and change of underwear
❐ light bag and good book
❐ small suitcase and nice outfit
❐ all but the kitchen sink

For $4: If I had money to blow, I would choose:
❐ one glorious night in a luxury hotel
❐ a weekend in a nice hotel
❐ a full week in a cheap motel
❐ two weeks camping in the boondocks

Habits

For $1: I am more likely to squeeze the toothpaste:
❏ in the middle   ❏ from the end

For $2: If I am lost, I will probably:
❏ stop and ask directions
❏ check the map
❏ find the way by driving around

For $3: I read the newspaper starting with the:
❏ front page
❏ funnies
❏ sports
❏ entertainment section

For $4: When I undress at night, I put my clothes:
❏ on a hanger in the closet
❏ folded neatly over a chair
❏ into a hamper or clothes basket
❏ on the floor

Food

For $1: I prefer to eat at a:
❏ fast-food restaurant
❏ fancy restaurant

For $2: On the menu, I look for something:
❏ familiar
❏ different
❏ way-out

For $3: When eating chicken, my preference is a:
❏ drumstick
❏ wing
❏ breast
❏ gizzard

For $4: I draw the line when it comes to eating:
❏ frog legs
❏ snails
❏ raw oysters
❏ Rocky Mountain oysters

Shows

For $1: I am more likely to:
❏ go see a first-run movie
❏ rent a video at home

For $2: On TV, my first choice is:
❏ news
❏ sports
❏ sitcoms

For $3: If a show gets scary, I will usually:
❏ go to the restroom
❏ close my eyes
❏ clutch a friend
❏ love it

For $4: In movies, I prefer:
❏ romantic comedies
❏ serious drama
❏ action films
❏ Disney animation

Work

For $1: I prefer to work at a job that is:
❏ too big to handle
❏ too small to be challenging

For $2: The job I find most unpleasant is:
❏ cleaning the house
❏ working in the yard
❏ balancing the checkbook

For $3: In choosing a job, I look for:
❏ salary
❏ security
❏ fulfillment
❏ working conditions

For $4: If I had to choose between these jobs, I would choose:
❏ pickle inspector at processing plant
❏ complaint officer at department store
❏ bedpan changer at hospital
❏ personnel manager in charge of firing

Let Me Tell You About My Day

What was your day like today? Use one of the characters below to help you describe your day to the group. Feel free to elaborate.

GREEK TRAGEDY
It was classic, not a dry eye in the house.

EPISODE OF THREE STOOGES
I was Larry, trapped between Curly and Moe.

SOAP OPERA
I didn't think these things could happen, until it happened to me.

ACTION ADVENTURE
When I rode onto the scene, everybody noticed.

BIBLE EPIC
Cecil B. DeMille couldn't have done it any better.

LATE NIGHT NEWS
It might as well have been broadcast over the airwaves.

BORING LECTURE
The biggest challenge of the day was staying awake.

PROFESSIONAL WRESTLING MATCH
I feel as if Hulk Hogan's been coming after me.

FIREWORKS DISPLAY
It was spectacular.

Music in My Life

Put an *"X"* on each of the lines below—somewhere between the two extremes—to indicate how you are feeling right now about each area of your life. If time is limited, choose only two or three:

IN MY PERSONAL LIFE, I'M FEELING LIKE ...
Blues in the Night_____ Feeling Groovy

IN MY FAMILY LIFE, I'M FEELING LIKE ...
Stormy Weather _____ The Sound of Music

IN MY EMOTIONAL LIFE, I'M FEELING LIKE ...
The Feeling Is Gone _____ On Eagle's Wings

IN MY WORK, SCHOOL OR CAREER, I'M FEELING LIKE ...
Take This Job and Shove It _____ The Future's So Bright I Gotta Wear Shades

IN MY SPIRITUAL LIFE, I'M FEELING LIKE ...
Sounds of Silence _____ Hallelujah Chorus

My Childhood Table

Try to recall the table where you ate most of your meals as a child, and the people who sat around that table. Use the questions below to describe these significant relationships, and how they helped to shape the person you are today.

1. What was the shape of the table?
2. Where did you sit?
3. Who else was at the table?
4. If you had to describe each person with a color, what would be the color of (for instance):
   - ❏ Your father? (e.g., dark blue, because he was conservative like IBM)
   - ❏ Your mother? (e.g., light green, because she reminded me of springtime)
5. If you had to describe the atmosphere at the table with a color, what would you choose? (e.g., bright orange, because it was warm and light)
6. Who was the person at the table who praised you and made you feel special?
7. Who provided the spiritual leadership in your home?

Home Improvement

Take inventory of your own life. Bob Munger, in his booklet *My Heart—Christ's Home*, describes the areas of a person's life as the rooms of a house. Give yourself a grade on each room as follows, then share with the others your best and worst grade.

❏ A = excellent   ❏ C = passing, needs a little dusting
❏ B = good   ❏ D = passing, but needs a lot of improvement

LIBRARY: This room is in your mind—what you allow to go into it and come out of it. It is the "control room" of the entire house.

DINING ROOM: Appetites, desires; those things your mind and spirit feed on for nourishment.

DRAWING ROOM: This is where you draw close to God—seeking time with him daily, not just in times of distress or need.

WORKSHOP: This room is where your gifts, talents and skills are put to work for God—by the power of the Spirit.

RUMPUS ROOM: The social area of your life; the things you do to amuse yourself and others.

HALL CLOSET: The one secret place that no one knows about, but is a real stumbling block in your walk in the Spirit.

How Is It With Your Soul?

John Wesley, the founder of the Methodist Church, asked his "class meetings" to check in each week at their small group meeting with this question: "How is it with your soul?" To answer this question, choose one of these four allegories to explain the past week in your life:

WEATHER: For example: "This week has been mostly cloudy, with some thunderstorms at midweek. Right now, the weather is a little brighter ..."

MUSIC: For example: "This past week has been like heavy rock music—almost too loud. The sound seems to reverberate off the walls."

COLOR: For example: "This past week has been mostly fall colors—deep orange, flaming red and pumpkin."

SEASON OF THE YEAR: For example: "This past week has been like springtime. New signs of life are beginning to appear on the barren trees, and a few shoots of winter wheat are breaking through the frozen ground."

My Spiritual Journey

The half-finished sentences below are designed to help you share your spiritual story. Ask one person to finish all the sentences. Then move to the next person, etc. If you are short on time, have only one person tell their story in this session.

1. RELIGIOUS BACKGROUND: My spiritual story begins in my home as a child, where the religious training was ...

2. CHURCH: The church that I went to as a child was ...

3. SIGNIFICANT PERSON: The person who had the greatest influence on my spiritual formation was ...

4. PERSONAL ENCOUNTER: The first time God became more than just a name to me was when ...

5. JOURNEY: Since my personal encounter with God, my Christian life might be described as ...

6. PRESENT: On a scale from 1 to 10, I would describe my spiritual energy level right now as a ...

7. NEXT STEP: The thing I need to work on right now in my spiritual life is ...

Bragging Rights

Check your group for bragging rights in these categories.

❏ SPEEDING TICKETS: the person with the most speeding tickets
❏ BROKEN BONES: the person with the most broken bones
❏ STITCHES: the person with the most stitches
❏ SCARS: the person with the longest scar
❏ FISH OR GAME: the person who claims they caught the largest fish or killed the largest animal
❏ STUNTS: the person with the most death-defying story
❏ IRON: the person who can pump the most iron

Personal Habits

Go around and have everyone in your group finish the sentence on the first category by putting an "*X*" somewhere between the two extremes. (For instance, on HOUSE-WORK ... I would put myself closer to "Where's the floor?")

ON HOUSEWORK, I AM SOMEWHERE BETWEEN:
Eat off the floor_____Where's the floor?

ON COOKING, I AM SOMEWHERE BETWEEN:
Every meal is an act of worship_____Make it fast and hold the frills

ON EXERCISING, I AM SOMEWHERE BETWEEN:
Workout every morning_____Click the remote

ON SHOPPING, I AM SOMEWHERE BETWEEN:
Shop all day for a bargain_____Only the best

ON EATING, I AM SOMEWHERE BETWEEN:
You are what you eat_____Eat, drink and be merry

American Graffiti

If Hollywood made a movie about your life on the night of your high school prom, what would be needed? Let each person in your group have a few minutes to recall these details. If you have more than four or five in your group, ask everyone to choose two or three topics to talk about.

1. LOCATION: Where were you living?
2. WEIGHT: How much did you weigh—soaking wet?
3. PROM: Where was it held?
4. DATE: Who did you take?
5. CAR / TRANSPORTATION: How did you get there?
   (If you used a car, what was the model, year, color, condition?)
6. ATTIRE: What did you wear?
7. PROGRAM: What was the entertainment?
8. AFTERWARD: What did you do afterward?
9. HIGHLIGHT: What was the highlight of the evening?
10. HOMECOMING: If you could go back and visit your high school, who would you like to see?

Group Orchestra

Read out loud the first item and let everyone nominate the person in your group for this musical instrument in your group orchestra. Then, read aloud the next instrument, and call out another name, etc.

ANGELIC HARP: Soft, gentle, melodious, wooing with heavenly sounds.

OLD-FASHIONED WASHBOARD: Nonconforming, childlike and fun.

PLAYER PIANO: Mischievous, raucous, honky-tonk—delightfully carefree.

KETTLEDRUM: Strong, vibrant, commanding when needed but usually in the background.

PASSIONATE CASTANET: Full of Spanish fervor—intense and always upbeat.

STRADIVARIUS VIOLIN: Priceless, exquisite, soul-piercing—with the touch of the master.

FLUTTERING FLUTE: Tender, lighthearted, wide-ranging and clear as crystal.

SCOTTISH BAGPIPES: Forthright, distinctive and unmistakable.

SQUARE DANCE FIDDLE: Folksy, down-to-earth, toe-tapping—sprightly and full of energy.

ENCHANTING OBOE: Haunting, charming, disarming—even the cobra is harmless with this sound.

MELLOW CELLO: Deep, sonorous, compassionate—adding body and depth to the orchestra.

PIPE ORGAN: Grand, magnificent, rich—versatile and commanding.

HERALDING TRUMPET: Stirring, lively, invigorating—signaling attention and attack.

CLASSICAL GUITAR: Contemplative, profound, thoughtful *and* thought-provoking.

ONE-MAN BAND: Able to do many things well, all at once.

COMB AND TISSUE PAPER: Makeshift, original, uncomplicated—homespun and creative.

SWINGING TROMBONE: Warm, rich—great in solo or background support.

Broadway Show

Imagine for a moment that your group has been chosen to produce a Broadway show, and you had to choose people from your group for all of the jobs for this production. Have someone read out loud the job description for the first job below—PRODUCER. Then, let everyone in your group call out the name of the person in your group who would best fit this job. (You don't have to agree.) Then read the job description for the next job and let everyone nominate another person, etc. You only have 10 minutes for this assignment, so move fast.

PRODUCER: Typical Hollywood business tycoon; extravagant, big-budget, big-production magnate in the Steven Spielberg style.

DIRECTOR: Creative, imaginative brains who coordinates the production and draws the best out of others.

HEROINE: Beautiful, captivating, everybody's heart throb; defenseless when men are around, but nobody's fool.

HERO: Tough, macho, champion of the underdog, knight in shining armor; defender of truth.

COMEDIAN: Childlike, happy-go-lucky, outrageously funny, keeps everyone laughing.

CHARACTER PERSON: Rugged individualist, outrageously different, colorful, adds spice to any surrounding.

FALL GUY: Easy-going, nonchalant character who wins the hearts of everyone by being the "foil" of the heavy characters.

TECHNICAL DIRECTOR: The genius for "sound and lights"; creates the perfect atmosphere.

COMPOSER OF LYRICS: Communicates in music what everybody understands; heavy into feelings, moods, outbursts of energy.

PUBLICITY AGENT: Advertising and public relations expert; knows all the angles, good at one-liners, a flair for "hot" news.

VILLAIN: The "bad guy" who really is the heavy for the plot, forces others to think, challenges traditional values; out to destroy anything artificial or hypocritical.

AUTHOR: Shy, aloof; very much in touch with feelings, sensitive to people, puts into words what others only feel.

STAGEHAND: Supportive, behind-the-scenes person who makes things run smoothly; patient and tolerant.

Wild Predictions

Try to match the people in your group to the crazy forecasts below. (Don't take it too seriously; it's meant to be fun!) Read out loud the first item and ask everyone to call out the name of the person who is most likely to accomplish this feat. Then, read the next item and ask everyone to make a new prediction, etc.

THE PERSON IN OUR GROUP MOST LIKELY TO ...

Be the used-car salesperson of the year

Replace Regis Philbin on *Regis and Kathie Lee*

Replace Vanna White on *Wheel of Fortune*

Rollerblade across the country

Open a charm school for Harley-Davidson bikers

Discover a new use for underarm deodorant

Run a dating service for lonely singles

Rise to the top in the CIA

Appear on the cover of *Muscle & Fitness Magazine*

Win the Iditarod dogsled race in Alaska

Make a fortune on pay toilet rentals

Write a best-selling novel based on their love life

Get listed in the *Guinness Book of World Records* for marathon dancing

Win the blue ribbon at the state fair for best Rocky Mountain oyster recipe

Bungee jump off the Golden Gate Bridge

Be the first woman to win the Indianapolis 500

Win the *MAD Magazine* award for worst jokes

Career Placements

Read the list of career choices aloud and quickly choose someone in your group for each job—based upon their unique gifts and talents. Have fun!

SPACE ENVIRONMENTAL ENGINEER: in charge of designing the bathrooms on space shuttles

SCHOOL BUS DRIVER: for junior high kids in New York City (earplugs supplied)

WRITER: of an "advice to the lovelorn" column in Hollywood

SUPERVISOR: of a complaint department for a large automobile dealership and service department

ANIMAL PSYCHIATRIST: for French poodles in a fashionable suburb of Paris

RESEARCH SCIENTIST: studying the fertilization patterns of the dodo bird—now extinct

SAFARI GUIDE: in the heart of Africa—for wealthy widows and eccentric bachelors

LITTLE LEAGUE BASEBALL COACH: in Mudville, Illinois—last year's record was 0 and 12

MANAGER: of your local McDonald's during the holiday rush with 210 teenage employees

LIBRARIAN: for the Walt Disney Hall of Fame memorabilia

CHOREOGRAPHER: for the Dallas Cowboys cheerleaders

NURSE'S AIDE: at a home for retired Sumo wrestlers

SECURITY GUARD: crowd control officer at a rock concert

ORGANIZER: of paperwork for Congress

PUBLIC RELATIONS MANAGER: for Dennis Rodman

BODYGUARD: for Rush Limbaugh on a speaking tour of feminist groups

TOY ASSEMBLY PERSON: for a toy store over the holidays

You and Me, Partner

Think of the people in your group as you read over the list of activities below. If you had to choose someone from your group to be your partner, who would you choose to do these activities with? Jot down each person's name beside the activity. You can use each person's name only once and you have to use everyone's name once—so think it through before you jot down their names. Then, let one person listen to what others chose for them. Then, move to the next person, etc., around your group.

WHO WOULD YOU CHOOSE FOR THE FOLLOWING?

_____ ENDURANCE DANCE CONTEST partner

_____ BOBSLED RACE partner for the Olympics

_____ TRAPEZE ACT partner

_____ MY UNDERSTUDY for my debut in a Broadway musical

_____ BEST MAN or MAID OF HONOR at my wedding

_____ SECRET UNDERCOVER AGENT copartner

_____ BODYGUARD for me when I strike it rich

_____ MOUNTAIN CLIMBING partner in climbing Mt. Everest

_____ ASTRONAUT to fly the space shuttle while I walk in space

_____ SAND CASTLE TOURNAMENT building partner

_____ PIT CREW foreman for entry in Indianapolis 500

_____ AUTHOR for my biography

_____ SURGEON to operate on me for a life-threatening cancer

_____ NEW BUSINESS START-UP partner

_____ TAG-TEAM partner for a professional wrestling match

_____ HEAVY-DUTY PRAYER partner

My Gourmet Group

Here's a chance to pass out some much deserved praise for the people who have made your group something special. Ask one person to sit in silence while the others explain the delicacy you would choose to describe the contribution this person has made to your group. Repeat the process for each member of the group.

CAVIAR: That special touch of class and aristocratic taste that has made the rest of us feel like royalty.

PRIME RIB: Stable, brawny, macho, the generous mainstay of any menu; juicy, mouth-watering "perfect cut" for good nourishment.

IMPORTED CHEESE: Distinctive, tangy, mellow with age; adds depth to any meal.

VINEGAR AND OIL: Tart, witty, dry; a rare combination of healing ointment and pungent spice to add "bite" to the salad.

ARTICHOKE HEARTS: Tender and disarmingly vulnerable; whets the appetite for heartfelt sharing.

FRENCH PASTRY: Tempting, irresistible "creme de la creme" dessert; the connoisseur's delight for topping off a meal.

PHEASANT UNDER GLASS: Wild, totally unique, a rare dish for people who appreciate original fare.

CARAFE OF WINE: Sparkling, effervescent, exuberant and joyful; outrageously free and liberating to the rest of us.

ESCARGOT AND OYSTERS: Priceless treasures of the sea once out of their shells; succulent, delicate and irreplaceable.

FRESH FRUIT: Vine-ripened, energy-filled, invigorating; the perfect treat after a heavy meal.

ITALIAN ICE CREAMS: Colorful, flavorful, delightfully childlike; the unexpected surprise in our group.

Thank You

How would you describe your experience with this group? Choose one of the animals below that best describes how your experience in this group affected your life. Then share your responses with the group.

WILD EAGLE: You have helped to heal my wings, and taught me how to soar again.

TOWERING GIRAFFE: You have helped me to hold my head up and stick my neck out, and reach over the fences I have built.

PLAYFUL PORPOISE: You have helped me to find a new freedom and a whole new world to play in.

COLORFUL PEACOCK: You have told me that I'm beautiful; I've started to believe it, and it's changing my life.

SAFARI ELEPHANT: I have enjoyed this new adventure, and I'm not going to forget it, or this group; I can hardly wait for the next safari.

LOVABLE HIPPOPOTAMUS: You have let me surface and bask in the warm sunshine of God's love.

LANKY LEOPARD: You have helped me to look closely at myself and see some spots, and you still accept me the way I am.

DANCING BEAR: You have taught me to dance in the midst of pain, and you have helped me to reach out and hug again.

ALL-WEATHER DUCK: You have helped me to celebrate life—even in stormy weather—and to sing in the rain.

Academy Awards

You have had a chance to observe the gifts and talents of the members of your group. Now you will have a chance to pass out some much deserved praise for the contribution that each member of the group has made to your life. Read out loud the first award. Then let everyone nominate the person they feel is the most deserving for that award. Then read the next award, etc., through the list. Have fun!

SPARK PLUG AWARD: for the person who ignited the group

DEAR ABBY AWARD: for the person who cared enough to listen

ROYAL GIRDLE AWARD: for the person who supported us

WINNIE THE POOH AWARD: for the warm, caring person when someone needed a hug

ROCK OF GIBRALTER AWARD: for the person who was strong in the tough times of our group

OPRAH AWARD: for the person who asked the fun questions that got us to talk

TED KOPPEL AWARD: for the person who asked the heavy questions that made us think

KING ARTHUR'S AWARD: for the knight in shining armor

PINK PANTHER AWARD: for the detective who made us deal with Scripture

NOBEL PEACE PRIZE: for the person who harmonized our differences of opinion without diminishing anyone

BIG MAC AWARD: for the person who showed the biggest hunger for spiritual things

SERENDIPITY CROWN: for the person who grew the most spiritually during the course—in your estimation

You Remind Me of Jesus

Every Christian reflects the character of Jesus in some way. As your group has gotten to know each other, you can begin to see how each person demonstrates Christ in their very own personality. Go around the circle and have each person listen while others take turns telling that person what they notice in him or her that reminds them of Jesus. You may also want to tell them why you selected what you did.

YOU REMIND ME OF ...

JESUS THE HEALER: You seem to be able to touch someone's life with your compassion and help make them whole.

JESUS THE SERVANT: There's nothing that you wouldn't do for someone.

JESUS THE PREACHER: You share your faith in a way that challenges and inspires people.

JESUS THE LEADER: As Jesus had a plan for the disciples, you are able to lead others in a way that honors God.

JESUS THE REBEL: By doing the unexpected, you remind me of Jesus' way of revealing God in unique, surprising ways.

JESUS THE RECONCILER: Like Jesus, you have the ability to be a peacemaker between others.

JESUS THE TEACHER: You have a gift for bringing light and understanding to God's Word.

JESUS THE CRITIC: You have the courage to say what needs to be said, even if it isn't always popular.

JESUS THE SACRIFICE: Like Jesus, you seem willing to sacrifice anything to glorify God.

Reflections

Take some time to evaluate the life of your group by using the statements below. Read the first sentence out loud and ask everyone to explain where they would put a dot between the two extremes. When you are finished, go back and give your group an overall grade in the category of Group Building, Bible Study and Mission.

GROUP BUILDING

On celebrating life and having fun together, we were more like a ...
wet blanket _____ hot tub

On becoming a caring community, we were more like a ...
prickly pear _____ cuddly teddy bear

BIBLE STUDY

On sharing our spiritual stories, we were more like a ...
shallow pond _____ spring-fed lake

On digging into Scripture, we were more like a ...
slow-moving snail _____ voracious anteater

MISSION

On inviting new people into our group, we were more like a ...
barbed-wire fence _____ wide-open door

On stretching our vision for mission, we were more like an ...
ostrich _____ eagle

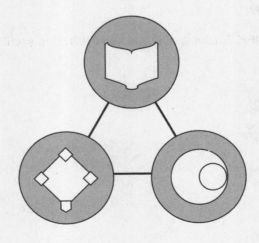

Human Bingo / Party Mixer

After the leader says "Go!" circulate the room, asking people the things described in the boxes. If someone answers "Yes" to a question, have them sign their initials in that box. Continue until someone completes the entire card—or one row if you don't have that much time. You can only use someone's name twice, and you cannot use your own name on your card.

can juggle	TP'd a house	never used an outhouse	sings in the shower	rec'd 6+ traffic tickets	paddled in school	watches Sesame Street
sleeps in church regularly	never changed a diaper	split pants in public	milked a cow	born out of the country	has been to Hawaii	can do the splits
watches soap operas	can touch tongue to nose	rode a motor-cycle	never ridden a horse	moved twice last year	sleeps on a waterbed	has hole in sock
walked in wrong restroom	loves classical music	skipped school	**FREE**	broke a leg	has a hot tub	loves eating sushi
is an only child	loves raw oysters	has a 3-inch + scar	doesn't wear PJ's	smoked a cigar	can dance the Charleston	weighs under 110 lbs.
likes writing poetry	still has tonsils	loves crossword puzzles	likes bubble baths	wearing Fruit of the Loom	doesn't use mouth-wash	often watches cartoons
kissed on first date	can wiggle ears	can play the guitar	plays chess regularly	reads the comics first	can touch palms to floor	sleeps with stuffed animal

Group Covenant

Any group can benefit from creating a group covenant. Reserve some time during one of the first meetings to discuss answers to the following questions. When everyone in the group has the same expectations for the group, everything runs more smoothly.

1. The purpose of our group is:

2. The goals of our group are:

3. We will meet for _____ weeks, after which we will decide if we wish to continue as a group. If we do decide to continue, we will reconsider this covenant.

4. We will meet _____ (weekly, every other week, monthly).

5. Our meetings will be from _____ o'clock to _____ o'clock, and we will strive to start and end on time.

6. We will meet at _____ or rotate from house to house.

7. We will take care of the following details: ☐ child care   ☐ refreshments

8. We agree to the following rules for our group:

    ☐ PRIORITY: While we are in this group, group meetings have priority.

    ☐ PARTICIPATION: Everyone is given the right to their own opinion and all questions are respected.

    ☐ CONFIDENTIALITY: Anything said in the meeting is not to be repeated outside the meeting.

    ☐ EMPTY CHAIR: The group stays open to new people and invites prospective members to visit the group.

    ☐ SUPPORT: Permission is given to call each other in times of need.

    ☐ ADVICE GIVING: Unsolicited advice is not allowed.

    ☐ MISSION: We will do all that is in our power to start a new group.

sizes the fact that in the incarnation Christ entered the stream of human life as a slave, that is, as a person without advantage, with no rights or privileges of his own for the express purpose of placing himself completely at the service of all mankind" (Hawthorne).

being made. In contrast to the verb in verse 6 (which stresses Christ's eternal nature), this verb points to the fact that at a particular time he was born in the likeness of a human being.

human likeness. The point is not that Jesus just seemed to be human. He assumed the identity of a person and was similar in all ways to other human beings.

2:8 *in appearance as a man.* The word translated "in appearance" is *schema,* and denotes that which is outward and changeable (over against *morphe,* which denotes that which is essential and eternal). In other words, Jesus was a true man, but only temporarily. As Barclay puts it: "He is essentially divine; but he was for a time human. His mankind was utterly real, but it was something which passed: the godhead was also utterly real, but it is something which abides forever."

he humbled himself. This is the central point that Paul wants to make. This is why he offered this illustration. Jesus is the ultimate model of one who lived a life of self-sacrifice, self-renunciation, and self-surrender. Jesus existed at the pinnacle and yet descended to the very base. There has never been a more radical humbling. Furthermore, this was not something forced upon Jesus. This was voluntarily chosen by Christ. It was not compelled by circumstances.

obedient to death. The extent of this humbling is defined by this clause. Jesus humbled himself to the furthest point one can go. He submitted to death itself for the sake of both God and humanity. There was no more dramatic way to demonstrate humility.

death on a cross. This was no ordinary death. For one thing, it came about in an unusually cruel way. Crucifixion was a harsh, demeaning and utterly painful way to die. For another thing, according to the Old Testament, those who died by hanging on a tree were considered to have been cursed by God.

For a Jew there was no more humiliating way to die. Jesus, who was equal to God, died like an accused criminal. His descent from glory had brought him as low as one could go.

> *Jesus Christ is "Lord." This is the name that was given to Jesus; the name that reflects who he really is. This is the name of God. Jesus is the supreme Sovereign of the universe.*

2:9 The self-humiliation of Jesus is followed by the God-induced exaltation of Jesus. Jesus descended to the depths and was raised to the heights.

name. In the ancient world, a name was more than just a way of distinguishing one individual from another. It revealed the inner nature or character of a person. The name given the resurrected Jesus is the supreme name—the name above all names—because this is who Jesus is in his innermost being.

2:10 *Jesus.* It is significant that the one before whom all will bow is Jesus, the man from Nazareth. The cosmic Lord is none other than the person who walked the roads of Palestine and talked to the people of Israel. He had a hometown, a family, a trade, and disciples. The one before whom Christians will stand at the Last Judgment is not an anonymous Life Force, but the man of Galilee who has a familiar face.

bow. Everyone will one day pay homage to Jesus. This worship will come from all of creation—all angels (in heaven), all people (on earth), and all demons (under the earth).

2:11 *Jesus Christ is Lord.* The climax of this hymn. This is the earliest and most basic confession of faith on the part of the church (see Acts 2:36; Rom. 10:9; 1 Cor. 12:3).

Lord. This is the name that was given to Jesus; the name that reflects who he really is (see v. 9). This is the name of God. Jesus is the supreme Sovereign of the universe.

6 Shining as Stars—Phil. 2:12–18

THREE-PART AGENDA

ICE-BREAKER	**BIBLE STUDY**	**CARING TIME**
15 Minutes	30 Minutes	15–45 Minutes

 LEADER: If you haven't already, now is the time to begin the process of identifying an Apprentice / Leader to start a new small group (see page M6 in the center section). Check the list of ice-breakers on page M7, especially if you have a new person in this session.

TO BEGIN THE BIBLE STUDY TIME
(Choose 1 or 2)

1. If you receive poor service in a restaurant, how likely are you to complain?

2. As a child, would you describe yourself as strong-willed or compliant?

3. How would you describe yourself now—strong-willed or compliant?

READ SCRIPTURE & DISCUSS
(If you don't have time for all the questions in this section, conclude the Bible Study [30 min.] by answering question #7.)

1. Who does Paul sound like in this passage: Your boss? An army sergeant? A coach at halftime?

2. What does it mean to "work out your salvation" (see note, "continue to work out your salvation," on v. 12)? Is salvation dependent on our works?

3. What is God's responsibility and what is yours for achieving God's "good purpose" (vv. 12–13; see notes on v. 13)?

Shining as Stars

[12]*Therefore, my dear friends, as you have always obeyed—not only in my presence, but now much more in my absence—continue to work out your salvation with fear and trembling,* [13]*for it is God who works in you to will and to act according to his good purpose.*

[14]*Do everything without complaining or arguing,* [15]*so that you may become blameless and pure, children of God without fault in a crooked and depraved generation, in which you shine like stars in the universe* [16]*as you hold out*[a] *the word of life—in order that I may boast on the day of Christ that I did not run or labor for nothing.* [17]*But even if I am being poured out like a drink offering on the sacrifice and service coming from your faith, I am glad and rejoice with all of you.* [18]*So you too should be glad and rejoice with me.*

[a]16 Or *hold on to*

4. What task is the most difficult for you to do without complaining or arguing?

5. If Paul were around today, what would he think about the moral values in this generation? About the moral standards in the Christian community?

6. On a scale of 1 (dim flashlight) to 10 (bright star), how brightly do you "shine" in your "universe"?

7. What is something God is doing for which this group can be glad and rejoice?

CARING TIME
(Choose 1 or 2 of these questions before taking prayer requests and closing in prayer. Be sure to pray for the empty chair.)

1. How effective has your group been in "shining like stars" when it comes to seeing new people join the group?

2. What is something you feel God is challenging you to do?

3. How can the group support you in prayer this week?

Summary. Paul ends this section (which began in 1:27) with an exhortation to the Philippians that they obey him by doing what he has been urging them to do—namely, they must forsake selfishness, conceit, pride, grumbling, and argument. These are the attitudes that have led to the disunity that now threatens their whole community. Instead, they must work at bringing health ("salvation") to their church. He encourages them in this task by reminding them that God is already at work in them, providing both the desire and the ability to do this. When they live the way they should—as blameless, pure and faultless children of God—they are like stars in the sky. Their lives stand in sharp contrast to the blackness of the world they inhabit. Furthermore, their efforts will be a fit sacrifice to God, as they are combined with the sacrifices Paul has made on their behalf.

2:12 Therefore. By this word, Paul signals that he is about to conclude the exhortations which he began back in 1:27.

my dear friends. This is a single Greek word which means literally, "beloved." By this phrase Paul indicates that he is not simply issuing commands to those who are under his authority. Instead, what he has to say is by way of injunctions to those whom he loves (his friends) given with their best interests in mind.

obeyed. Paul links the hymn about Jesus to the experience of the Philippians via the word "obey." Just as Christ was obedient even to death (2:8) so too they should obey his apostolic injunctions. Such obedience ought not to be distasteful to the Philippians since they have "always obeyed." The word "obey" carries with it the idea of "hearing" and then "submitting" to what is heard.

not only in my presence but ... in my absence. Once again, as in 1:27, Paul makes reference to the fact that they ought to live out a Christian lifestyle not just when he (or some other leader) is on the scene but at all times.

continue to work out your salvation. This is what Paul commands them to do. To understand what he is urging on them, it is important to understand how the word "salvation" is used here. The Greek word translated "salvation" has several meanings in the

New Testament. It can refer to the saving work of God in the life of a Christian which begins here and now and is completed on the Day of Judgment. This word can also mean "health and wholeness." The context of this verse indicates that Paul is thinking of the whole community and not the individual Christian. (His point in this passage is that they must get over their self-centeredness and heal the divisions in the church by developing a unity based on concern for others.) Furthermore, the word "your" is plural. Thus the broader sense of the Greek word is probably intended. Paul is concerned with "the restoration of the health and spiritual well-being of the community" (Loh and Nida).

> *The Christian life is lived out when people work hard to achieve God's will, while simultaneously opening themselves to the power of God which promotes the same end.*

fear and trembling. This phrase can refer to that sense of awe which a creature feels when standing before the Creator, and which drives him or her to seek and to do the will of God. It can also refer to an attitude of obedience toward God.

2:13 it is God who works in you. The word for "works" is *energein,* from which the English word "energy" is derived. By this phrase Paul seeks to indicate that the power of God is already at work within the Philippian church. In order for spiritual harmony to come, they must therefore avail themselves of this power. In other words (taking this phrase and the previous one), what Paul is saying is that the Christian life is lived out when people work hard to achieve God's will, while simultaneously opening themselves to the power of God which promotes the same end. The Christian life is not an "either/or" situation—where we either work and struggle to be what God wants us to be, or we simply sit back and passively let God make us into what he wants. Instead it is a "both/and" situation, in which human and divine activity combine to produce the desired end.

to will and to act. God promotes both the desire to do his will and the drive necessary to accomplish it.

2:14 complaining. This is the same sort of mumbling and grumbling against the leaders of the community that characterized Israel in the wilderness (see Ex. 15:24).

arguing. This is useless and ill-tempered disputation (perhaps centering on the doctrines taught by false teachers). Both complaining and arguing create divisions within a community.

2:15 blameless / pure / without fault. A description of what the Philippians should strive to become. In relationship to the outside world, they are to be blameless; i.e., the kind of people against whom no accusation can be laid. In relationship to themselves, they are to be as pure as metal that is unmixed with an alloy (or wine that is unmixed with water). In relationship to God, they are to be as faultless as an unblemished sacrificial animal.

shine like stars. When they live this way, they will be like bright lights which illuminate a dark sky (the "crooked and depraved" generation in which they live).

2:16 word of life. The Gospel which Paul and they preached.

boast. Paul is responsible for all but four of the 50 times this word (in various forms) is used in the New Testament. By it he "does not mean a vanity that deserves condemnation but a deep exultation or proper pride that only the Philippians can provide Paul by their obedience to God's commands" (Hawthorne).

day of Christ. The Day of Judgment, when all people will stand before Christ. Since Christians will be called upon to give account of how well they used the gifts entrusted to them (see 1 Cor. 4:1–5), Paul urges the Philippians to continue to obey the demands of the Gospel.

run or labor. Paul describes his ministry by means of two metaphors. The image of "running" comes from the world of sports, and pictures an athlete straining to reach the finish line (see Gal. 2:2; Phil. 3:12–14). The second image comes from the world of work, and describes labor to the point of exhaustion. Both refer to the toil, training, effort, and discipline required to succeed in either sports or work. Paul fears that if the Philippians do not live in the way he urges, his great effort on their behalf will have been wasted. On the Day of Judgment, he will have nothing to show for all the effort he expended on them. He appeals to them as their friend and apostle not to let this happen. He wants to be able to "boast" about them at the judgment.

2:17 But. Paul hastens to point out the fact of their own "sacrifice and service," lest they feel that he is too critical of them (or that he has no confidence in them). Their past acts of love and service demonstrate their commitment.

poured out like a drink offering. His specific reference is to the practice of pouring out a libation (a glass of wine or olive oil) over the altar as a part of the sacrificial ritual. Thus, what he is saying here is that his faithful service, combined with their "sacrifice and service," form a fit offering to God.

2:18 Such lives of sacrifice to God ought to bring joy, in that Christians thereby know that they are walking in the way that God desires.

The Christian life is not an "either/or" situation—where we either work and struggle to be what God wants us to be, or we simply sit back and passively let God make us into what he wants. Instead it is a "both/and" situation, in which human and divine activity combine to produce the desired end.

7 Fellow Workers—Phil. 2:19–30

THREE-PART AGENDA

ICE-BREAKER
15 Minutes

BIBLE STUDY
30 Minutes

CARING TIME
15–45 Minutes

 LEADER: Have you started working with your group about your mission—for instance, by having them review page M3 in the center section? If you have a new person at the meeting, remember to do an appropriate ice-breaker from the center section.

TO BEGIN THE BIBLE STUDY TIME
(Choose 1 or 2)

1. When you were in grade school, who was your best friend? Why did you like this person so much?

2. In your first real job, what kind of boss did you have? What kind of employee were you?

3. If you were given a personal servant right now, how would you put them to work? How would you feel about having a personal servant?

READ SCRIPTURE & DISCUSS
(If you don't have time for all the questions in this section, conclude the Bible Study [30 min.] by answering question #8.)

1. Who is someone you trust to look after things for you when you are away from home?

2. From verses 19–24, what are two or three words you would use to describe Timothy?

3. From verses 25–30, what are two or three words you would use to describe Epaphroditus?

Timothy and Epaphroditus

¹⁹I hope in the Lord Jesus to send Timothy to you soon, that I also may be cheered when I receive news about you. ²⁰I have no one else like him, who takes a genuine interest in your welfare. ²¹For everyone looks out for his own interests, not those of Jesus Christ. ²²But you know that Timothy has proved himself, because as a son with his father he has served with me in the work of the gospel. ²³I hope, therefore, to send him as soon as I see how things go with me. ²⁴And I am confident in the Lord that I myself will come soon.

²⁵But I think it is necessary to send back to you Epaphroditus, my brother, fellow worker and fellow soldier, who is also your messenger, whom you sent to take care of my needs. ²⁶For he longs for all of you and is distressed because you heard he was ill. ²⁷Indeed he was ill, and almost died. But God had mercy on him, and not on him only but also on me, to spare me sorrow upon sorrow. ²⁸Therefore I am all the more eager to send him, so that when you see him again you may be glad and I may have less anxiety. ²⁹Welcome him in the Lord with great joy, and honor men like him, ³⁰because he almost died for the work of Christ, risking his life to make up for the help you could not give me.

4. Who is someone you know that models humble service to others?

5. What is the closest you have come to having a "spiritual parent" (see v. 22)? What is the closest you have come to having a "spiritual child"?

6. How free are you with your praise of others? How are you at receiving a compliment?

7. How would you want your friends in the faith to be able to describe you?

8. What service do you feel God has called you to do for his kingdom?

CARING TIME

(Choose 1 or 2 of these questions before taking prayer requests and closing in prayer. Be sure to pray for the empty chair.)

1. Have you started working on your group mission—to choose an Apprentice / Leader from your group to start a new group in the future? (See the Mission / Multiplication on page M3.)

2. How do the people in this group encourage you and refresh your spirits?

3. How can the group remember you in prayer this week?

Notes—Philippians 2:19–30

Summary. Paul begins a new section, in which he gives the Philippians news about two men who are important to them: Timothy and Epaphroditus. This is his second news-oriented passage (the first being his report on his own situation in 1:12–26). Although this is a new section and Paul has shifted his focus away from the problem of disunity in the Philippian church, what he says here is connected to the previous section. When discussing the kind of lifestyle that led to unity, Paul offered two examples of self-giving sacrifice. First, there was the unparalleled example of Jesus Christ, who, though he was God, became a servant of mankind. Second, Paul offers his own willingness to be "poured out like a drink offering" as another example of how they ought to be living. Now here he gives two more examples of men who lived in a self-sacrificial way. Timothy has demonstrated "a genuine interest in [their] welfare." And Epaphroditus "almost died for the work of Christ."

2:19 *I hope.* It is interesting to note that when he refers to his own plan to come to Philippi, Paul says, "I am confident in the Lord that I myself will come soon" (v. 24). But when he refers to his plan to send Timothy (vv. 19,23), he seems less certain ("I hope"). Perhaps Paul feels that since he is sure he will be released soon, it may not be necessary for Timothy to visit them.

in the Lord Jesus. Paul is not making these plans solely on the basis of his own will and desire. He is seeking to follow God's leading in this matter. This is a good example of the principle he just enunciated, whereby Christians are to live in the tension between actively working out their own salvation while simultaneously depending upon God to work his will in their lives (2:12–13).

Timothy. This is Paul's long-time friend and co-worker who was with him when he founded the church in Philippi. This is not the first time that Paul has sent Timothy on a mission. Previously, he sent Timothy to Thessalonica from Athens (1 Thess. 3:1–9) and to Corinth from Ephesus (1 Cor. 4:17; 16:10–11).

that I also may be cheered when I receive news about you. Paul has two reasons for sending Timothy. First, he knows that the news Timothy will bring back to him about their situation will cheer him greatly while he is confined in prison. (He anticipates that they will follow his advice and deal with their own disunity as well as rid themselves of the false teachers.) Second, by implication, Paul wants the Philippians to be cheered up when Timothy gives them the news of Paul's situation. (Paul says "that I also may be cheered," implying that the Philippians had already been cheered up.)

> *In the post-apostolic church, some Christians took Epaphroditus as their model. They called themselves "The Gamblers," and deliberately risked their lives for the sake of the Gospel. They visited prisons, cared for the sick (even those with contagious diseases), buried victims of the plague, etc.*

2:20 *like him.* This is a rare Greek word which means "of like mind" or "one who shares the same feelings." By using this word, Paul conveys the fact that Timothy comes in his name and speaks on his behalf. In other words, in hearing Timothy, they are hearing Paul.

a genuine interest in your welfare. Timothy is authentically and sincerely concerned about the welfare of the Philippians. This attitude of concern for others is what Paul is trying to engender in the Philippians (see 2:3–4).

2:21 In contrast to Timothy's attitude, there are others who are motivated by their own concerns and not by the concerns of Jesus Christ. Perhaps Paul is referring to those he mentioned in 1:15,27 who preach Christ but do so for their own ends. However, since he gives no other information it is not possible to pinpoint exactly the source of the distress to which he gives voice in this parenthetical comment.

2:22 *proved himself.* The Greek word used here indicates that Timothy has been tested in difficult situations and has come through them successfully.

as a son with his father. Timothy is more than a trusted colleague. He is a friend who has stood by Paul through thick and thin. He is, in fact, like a son to Paul. It is interesting that Paul uses the more affectionate word "child," instead of the normal word for "son."

served. This is literally, "served as a slave." Paul is careful to phrase this so as to indicate that it was the Gospel Timothy served, not he personally. ("He has served with me in the work of the gospel.")

2:23 The reason for Paul's delay in sending Timothy probably has to do with his need of Timothy to help him with personal affairs that he cannot attend to himself while he is in prison. Probably what Paul needs help with is his upcoming trial. He might also need Timothy to minister on his behalf in Rome, especially in the light of the controversy his presence in jail has created (see 1:15–17). This delay is probably not a matter of waiting until his trial is over so that Timothy can convey news of the outcome to the Philippians. Paul is quite confident that he will be released and then he will come himself to visit them (see v. 24).

2:25 *Epaphroditus.* Epaphroditus had been sent by the Philippian church to convey a gift to Paul, and then to stay on as a member of Paul's apostolic group. However, he fell ill. The church heard about this and became quite anxious about him. In addition, Epaphroditus was homesick. For both reasons, Paul senses that it is time for Epaphroditus to return to Philippi.

my brother. This is the first of five nouns in this verse which Paul uses to describe Epaphroditus. He is a genuine member of the family of God.

fellow worker. Paul uses this word to describe those who ministered alongside him.

fellow soldier. Epaphroditus assisted him in battles against the enemies of the Gospel.

your messenger. He was the envoy who brought gifts to Paul from them. This word is literally "apostle," the same term used by Paul to define his own office.

take care. This is a single Greek word and can be translated "minister." It was used by the Greeks as a title of honor bestowed upon those who rendered great service to their city at their own expense (such as staging a public drama or fitting out a battleship). Epaphroditus "ministered" to Paul.

2:26 Paul confirms that the rumor they heard was true: Epaphroditus did lay close to death. Paul goes on to say that his recovery (however it came—by healing or by natural processes) was due to God.

2:27 *sorrow upon sorrow.* The recovery of Epaphroditus spared Paul from literally "wave upon wave of grief." Although his own death might seem at times to be a gain for him (1:21–23), Paul was not immune to the sorrow that comes when friends die.

2:28 Paul gives two more reasons why he is sending back Epaphroditus—to provide the Philippians with a reason for rejoicing (by seeing that he is well) and to relieve his own anxiety. Why Paul would be less anxious when Epaphroditus returned is not clear. Perhaps then he would cease worrying about the health of his friend. Another possibility is that when Epaphroditus returned home the Philippians would have up-to-date information about Paul's own state of affairs and would thus cease worrying about him. Paul may also feel less anxious when he knows that Epaphroditus is on the spot helping to deal with the problems in the Philippian church.

2:30 *risking his life.* A gambling term, it denotes one who risked everything on the roll of the dice. In the post-apostolic church, some Christians took Epaphroditus as their model. They called themselves "The Gamblers," and deliberately risked their lives for the sake of the Gospel. They visited prisons, cared for the sick (even those with contagious diseases), buried victims of the plague, etc.

8 Knowing Christ—Philippians 3:1–11

THREE-PART AGENDA

ICE-BREAKER	BIBLE STUDY	CARING TIME
15 Minutes	30 Minutes	15–45 Minutes

 LEADER: To help you identify an Apprentice / Leader for a new small group (or if you have a new person at this meeting), see the listing of ice-breakers on page M7 of the center section.

TO BEGIN THE BIBLE STUDY TIME
(Choose 1 or 2)

1. Growing up, who was the bully you had to look out for?

2. What hobby or activity are you most enthusiastic about right now?

3. What is one accomplishment you are proud of?

READ SCRIPTURE & DISCUSS
(If you don't have time for all the questions in this section, conclude the Bible Study [30 min.] by answering question #8.)

1. During this past week, how did you do at rejoicing in the Lord?

2. Why is Paul so concerned about "those dogs"? What or who are the "dogs" in your life you have to watch out for?

3. What does "confidence in the flesh" mean: Good looks? Positive reputation? Education?

4. If someone with Paul's resume came to your group, how would you feel?

No Confidence in the Flesh

3 *Finally, my brothers, rejoice in the Lord! It is no trouble for me to write the same things to you again, and it is a safeguard for you.*

²Watch out for those dogs, those men who do evil, those mutilators of the flesh. ³For it is we who are the circumcision, we who worship by the Spirit of God, who glory in Christ Jesus, and who put no confidence in the flesh— ⁴though I myself have reasons for such confidence.

If anyone else thinks he has reasons to put confidence in the flesh, I have more: ⁵circumcised on the eighth day, of the people of Israel, of the tribe of Benjamin, a Hebrew of Hebrews; in regard to the law, a Pharisee; ⁶as for zeal, persecuting the church; as for legalistic righteousness, faultless.

⁷But whatever was to my profit I now consider loss for the sake of Christ. ⁸What is more, I consider everything a loss compared to the surpassing greatness of knowing Christ Jesus my Lord, for whose sake I have lost all things. I consider them rubbish, that I may gain Christ ⁹and be found in him, not having a righteousness of my own that comes from the law, but that which is through faith in Christ—the righteousness that comes from God and is by faith. ¹⁰I want to know Christ and the power of his resurrection and the fellowship of sharing in his sufferings, becoming like him in his death, ¹¹and so, somehow, to attain to the resurrection from the dead.

5. In his "profit and loss" accounting system (vv. 4–8), how does Paul ultimately figure the worth of his religious credentials?

6. According to Paul, what's the secret to success?

7. Paul desired to know Christ better. On a scale of 1 (low) to 10 (great), how does your desire in this area rank?

8. What is something you can do this week to know Christ in a more meaningful way?

CARING TIME

(Choose 1 or 2 of these questions before taking prayer requests and closing in prayer. Be sure to pray for the empty chair.)

1. What is your dream for the future mission of this group? (See page M3 in the center section.)

2. Is there something you would like this group to help hold you accountable for?

3. How would you like the group to pray for you this week?

Summary. Paul now turns his attention to the false teachers who are troubling the church at Philippi. First, he describes them by means of three rather vivid terms (dogs, evildoers, mutilators), each of which punctures in some way their image of themselves (v. 2). Then, he points out the error in their teaching. They are saying that it is by keeping the Law that one gains God's favor (v. 3). To demonstrate that righteousness is not attained in this way, Paul describes his own background (vv. 4–6). He was the most orthodox of Jews and yet when he met Jesus on the Damascus Road, he came to realize that all his accomplishments and all the privileges afforded him because of his heritage were mere rubbish in comparison to knowing Christ (vv. 7–11).

3:1 *Finally.* It appears that Paul is about to conclude his letter. But in verse 2 he suddenly goes off in a whole new direction and issues a strong warning about the false teachers in Philippi. When Paul started to dictate the conclusion of his letter, perhaps he remembered suddenly that he had not yet said anything about the enemies to which he had alluded in 1:28. So, he added this parenthetical warning before getting to his actual concluding remarks which begin at 4:8.

rejoice in the Lord. Paul continues to emphasize rejoicing. Here for the first time he adds the words "in the Lord."

safeguard. Joy is a safeguard against those negative attitudes that bring disunity. A person who is rejoicing cannot simultaneously be grumbling or promoting his or her own interests.

3:2 By means of strong and even abusive language, Paul warns the Philippians about the false teachers who oppose them. The exact identity of these opponents is impossible to pin down. (One scholar notes that no less that 18 different identities have been proposed for these enemies of the Gospel.)

dogs. A derogatory term used by Jews in the first century to describe Gentiles, given its force by the fact that Jews despised dogs (which they considered "unclean"). They are, in fact, the real "dogs" because of the way in which they are perverting the truth of God.

men who do evil. The Jews considered themselves to be the only people who did good in the eyes of God. But once again, Paul turns their self-image upside down and contends that, in fact, they are really evildoers (because they rely on their good works for their righteousness instead of on God's grace).

mutilators of the flesh. In Greek, this is a pun that is difficult to translate. Paul is saying that their circumcision is really mutilation. Not only is it of no value, but it actually goes against God's will.

> *Joy is a safeguard against those negative attitudes that bring disunity. A person who is rejoicing cannot simultaneously be grumbling or promoting his or her own interests.*

3:3 *we who worship by the Spirit of God.* This is the first of three phrases in verse 3 by which Paul demonstrates that the Christians have become the *true* circumcision. Judaism had become a religion of external ritual, whereas Christian worship was not so much governed by law as it was by the inner promptings of the Spirit.

who glory in Christ Jesus. Jews prided themselves in the Law and their observance of it, while Christians "boast" (the literal meaning of "glory") of Jesus who has brought them righteousness.

who put no confidence in the flesh. Here the word "flesh" probably means "unredeemed human nature." Christians do not rely upon personal striving as the basis for their righteousness.

3:4–11 Paul anticipates the response of these Jewish enemies: "You say all this, Paul, because you are a Christian and not an authentic Jew." To answer this charge, Paul lays out before them his substantial credentials as a Jew (vv. 4–6), and then points out that such accomplishments lack any value when it comes to obtaining the favor of God (vv. 7–11).

3:4 *confidence in the flesh*. This is what these Jews are promoting: a righteousness based on heritage and accomplishment.

3:5 *eighth day*. It was on the eighth day after birth that a Jewish child (as opposed to a proselyte) was circumcised. Paul was a true Jew right from the time of his birth.

***the tribe of Benjamin*.** The members of the tribe of Benjamin constituted an elite group within Israel.

***a Pharisee*.** He was one of the spiritual elite in Israel.

3:6 *as for zeal, persecuting the church*. Zeal was a highly prized virtue among the Jews. Paul had demonstrated his zeal for the Law by ferreting out Christians and bringing them to trial (see Acts 22:4–5; 26:9–11).

***faultless*.** To the best of his ability, Paul tried to observe the whole Law. Taken together, all these attributes mean that Paul was in every way the match of his opponents in Philippi. He had lived at the very pinnacle of Judaism.

3:7 *But*. When looked at from one point of view, Paul would appear to have been a highly-privileged, highly-accomplished religious leader. But when looked at from another point of view, this so-called advantage is seen to be mere illusion.

***profit / loss*.** Paul describes his change in outlook in terms of a balance sheet. What was once on the "profit" side of the ledger (when he was a Pharisee) has been shifted over to the "loss" side (now that he is a Christian).

***for the sake of Christ*.** When Paul met the resurrected Jesus, his whole way of looking at himself and God changed radically. He saw that his zeal had, in fact, driven him to kill people (so that he was guilty before God, and not righteous as he had assumed). He also saw that his view of what God wanted was wrong (God did not desire conformity to the Law, but rather trust in Christ).

3:8 *compared to*. Paul discovered that only one thing had any ultimate value—knowing Christ Jesus—and knowing Christ did not come as a result of personal accomplishment.

***knowing Christ*.** "Primarily, this knowledge is not intellectual but experiential. In this context, the knowledge of Christ is personal and intimate, as the expression my Lord shows, certainly more than an intellectual apprehension of truth about Christ. Rather, it is a personal appropriation of and communion with Christ himself. The knowledge of Christ Jesus no doubt does involve one's thought, but in its distinctive biblical usage it may be said to involve primarily one's heart" (Loh and Nida).

***rubbish*.** This is really quite a vulgar term, and refers to either "waste food bound for the garbage pit" or "human dung."

3:8c–10 Paul identifies the three reasons why he counts his former privileges as mere "dung." They were useless in his desire to "gain Christ," to "be found in him" (and so possess true righteousness), and to "know Christ and the power of his resurrection."

3:10 *know*. The knowledge about which Paul speaks is personal knowledge (i.e., to "know" someone as intimately as a wife "knows" a husband) and not just intellectual knowledge (i.e., knowing "about" someone).

***the power of his resurrection*.** Paul wants to experience personally the resurrected Christ in all his power (Eph. 1:18–21).

***becoming like him*.** Paul coins a new word by which he expresses "the staggering idea that he and all believers are caught up into Christ and are indissolubly linked together with him to share with him in all the events of his life, including his death and resurrection ..." (Hawthorne).

3:11 Although believers experience in the here-and-now the power of the Resurrection, there also awaits them a future resurrection (when they will be free from sin and its consequences).

***somehow, to attain*.** In humility, he expresses his sense that it is solely by God's grace that he would gain such a gift.

9 Pressing On—Philippians 3:12–4:1

THREE-PART AGENDA

ICE-BREAKER	BIBLE STUDY	CARING TIME
15 Minutes	30 Minutes	15–45 Minutes

 LEADER: *To help you identify people who might form the core of a new small group (or if a new person comes to this meeting), see the listing of ice-breakers on page M7 of the center section.*

TO BEGIN THE BIBLE STUDY TIME
(Choose 1 or 2)

1. What's the best prize or award you've ever received?

2. At what point in your life did you consider yourself to be a grown-up?

3. What is one goal you have for yourself to accomplish in the next five years?

READ SCRIPTURE & DISCUSS
(If you don't have time for all the questions in this section, conclude the Bible Study [30 min.] by answering question #8.)

1. Using the imagery of a track race, where does Paul picture himself in his spiritual life (vv. 12–14)? What prize is he after?

2. Who do you look to as an example of Christian living? Who are you trying to be an example to?

3. In today's society, who would you say the "enemies of the cross" (v. 18) are?

4. What does it mean to you to be a citizen of heaven and an heir of God's kingdom?

Pressing on Toward the Goal

12Not that I have already obtained all this, or have already been made perfect, but I press on to take hold of that for which Christ Jesus took hold of me. 13Brothers, I do not consider myself yet to have taken hold of it. But one thing I do: Forgetting what is behind and straining toward what is ahead, 14I press on toward the goal to win the prize for which God has called me heavenward in Christ Jesus.

15All of us who are mature should take such a view of things. And if on some point you think differently, that too God will make clear to you. 16Only let us live up to what we have already attained.

17Join with others in following my example, brothers, and take note of those who live according to the pattern we gave you. 18For, as I have often told you before and now say again even with tears, many live as enemies of the cross of Christ. 19Their destiny is destruction, their god is their stomach, and their glory is in their shame. Their mind is on earthly things. 20But our citizenship is in heaven. And we eagerly await a Savior from there, the Lord Jesus Christ, 21who, by the power that enables him to bring everything under his control, will transform our lowly bodies so that they will be like his glorious body.

4 *Therefore, my brothers, you whom I love and long for, my joy and crown, that is how you should stand firm in the Lord, dear friends!*

5. What do you look forward to the most when you think about heaven?

6. During this past week, how much have you been weighed down by earthly circumstances? What would change if you lived next week as a citizen of heaven and an alien of the earth?

7. If you compared your spiritual life right now to a track race, where would you be: Sitting on the sidelines? Warming up? At the starting block? Giving it your all? Gutting it out? Giving up?

8. How can this group help you "stand firm in the Lord" (4:1) this week?

CARING TIME

(Choose 1 or 2 of these questions before taking prayer requests and closing in prayer. Be sure to pray for the empty chair.)

1. Who would you choose as the leader if your group "gave birth" to a new small group? Who else would you choose to be part of the leadership core for a new group?

2. Is there a spiritual struggle or victory from this last week you would like to share?

3. How can the group pray for you as you run the race of life?

Summary. In the previous unit Paul laid bare his heart to the Philippians. He described how in contrast to his former reliance on an impeccable heritage and on zealous striving to obey the Law, now his driving passion had become that of "knowing Christ." This is what motivated him. This is what consumed him. In this unit, he describes in more detail what it means to strive to take hold of Christ. Here he also warns against anyone who might feel

---

Christians are urged forward by what the future holds instead of simply running away from what they did in their past.

---

that they have already "arrived" spiritually and thus attained "perfection." Over against this pattern of striving to know Christ (vv. 12–14) which he enjoins the Philippians to follow (vv. 15–17), Paul sets the pattern modeled by the false teachers (vv. 18–19). Their concern is with food laws and circumcision— "earthly things"—in contrast to the heavenly kingdom to which Christians belong.

3:12 *Not that.* Paul disclaims that he has reached any sort of perfection in his spiritual life, or has fully comprehended who Christ is.

obtained. This is a difficult word to translate because it has such a wide range of meanings. It can be translated "to take hold of," "to apprehend," "to comprehend," as well as "to obtain." It probably refers to comprehending fully on a mental and spiritual level just who Jesus Christ is.

perfect. This is the only time in his epistles that Paul uses this word. He borrows it (probably) from the vocabulary of the mystery religions. They offered to devotees the "secret" that would enable them to attain a sort of blissful perfection which would end their earthly struggles. In contrast, Paul indicates that he has not yet fully understood Jesus Christ. There is simply too much to know of Christ ever to grasp it all this side of heaven. Thus the Jewish teachers are wrong when they say that if people are circumcised and keep the Law, they can attain perfection.

press on. In contrast to those groups that claim it is possible to attain spiritual perfection here and now, the Christian life is one of relentless striving to know Christ in his fullness.

to take hold of. This is another difficult word to translate. It can refer to winning a prize, as for example, in a race. Or it can mean to understand or comprehend something.

Jesus took hold of me. Paul refers here to his conversion experience on the Damascus Road.

3:13 *consider.* This word means "to calculate precisely." Paul means that after looking carefully at his life and all he has experienced of Christ, he has come to the conclusion that he has a long way to go in his spiritual pilgrimage.

Forgetting what is behind. In order to press on to a successful conclusion of his spiritual pilgrimage, Paul must first cease looking at his past. He must forget past failures (such as persecuting the church). He must also forget past successes (such as reaching the pinnacle of Jewish spirituality). Neither guilt nor personal attainment will assist him in gaining Christ.

what is ahead. If the first movement in the spiritual pilgrimage is to forget the past, the second movement is to concentrate totally on what lies ahead— full comprehension of Jesus Christ. Christians are urged forward by what the future holds instead of simply running away from what they did in their past.

3:14 *goal.* This is the mark on the track that signifies the end of the race.

the prize. What Paul seems to have in mind is the moment at the end of the race, when the winner is called forward by the games master to receive the victory palm or wreath. Likewise, on the day of resurrection, the Christian will be called forward by God to receive the prize, which is full knowledge of Christ Jesus.

3:15–16 Although some in Philippi consider themselves to have arrived at spiritual perfection, Paul knows that this is not possible. He also knows that such folk view this matter differently than he, and that they will not be convinced by what he says. However, Paul is confident that God will in time reveal the truth to them. In the meantime, he encourages them not to let these differences in understanding impede growth and harmony in the church.

:15 *mature.* This is the same word that is translated "perfect" in verse 12. He uses this word in a slightly ironic way here: "Those of us who might think we are 'perfect' know that there is no such thing as true perfection. There is only continual striving to comprehend Christ."

:17 *following my example.* Paul does not mean to imply that he has somehow attained the perfection they seek. On the contrary, he has already disavowed that. What he is calling them to imitate is his striving to find his goodness in Christ Jesus, his willingness to give himself sacrificially for the sake of others, and his deep passion to see the Gospel advanced (1:12–26; 3:7–11).

the pattern. Paul has defined the pattern for the Christian life as forgetting what is behind and constantly forging ahead to grasp the fullness of Jesus Christ on all levels of one's being.

3:18 *with tears.* These are tears of frustration on Paul's part, that his beloved countrymen continue to reject the Gospel.

enemies of the cross. It was the fact of Jesus' death that so scandalized the Jews. They found it almost impossible to accept that God could will and work through a crucified Messiah.

3:19 *destruction.* Since they reject the Cross (which lies at the heart of the way of salvation), their destiny is to live outside the life offered by God in Christ. "Thus, because these Jews reject out of hand the only one who can save them, preserve their souls, and give them life, there is nothing left but for them to experience the opposite—loss, destruction, death—the utter ruin of their lives" (Hawthorne).

their god is their stomach. The Jews were obsessed with laws relating to what they could eat and drink, how and when to eat, ritual preparation for eating, etc. A key feature of their religious life thus involved the issue of food.

shame. Probably refers to nakedness, and thus this is a reference to circumcision (which was another key feature of the Jewish religious life). In other words, food laws and circumcision had become gods to these people (Hawthorne).

3:20 *citizenship.* In contrast to the Jewish teachers whose focus is on "earthly things" (v. 19), the focus of Christians is on heaven (where their true home lies). This is a particularly appropriate image for the Philippians, who lived as citizens of Rome (and yet were a long distance from the mother city).

eagerly await. Paul captures the keen anticipation and happy expectation of the Christians who long for Christ's return, at which time they will be rescued from their trials and will experience new life in all its fullness.

3:21 *our lowly bodies.* In contrast to those who taught that perfection was possible here and now, Christians knew that it was only at the Second Coming, by the work of Christ, that their frail, weak and corrupt bodies would be transformed into a spiritual body akin to Christ's "glorious body."

> *The pattern for the Christian life is forgetting what is behind and constantly forging ahead to grasp the fullness of Jesus Christ on all levels of one's being.*

4:1 *Therefore.* This verse marks the transition to a new subject. Since Christians are members of the colony of heaven, and since they await transformation into something glorious, therefore—this is what Paul calls upon them to do—they are to "stand firm" in their faith and not be tempted away by the teachings of these Jewish missionaries.

crown. This is the wreath of wild olive leaves laced with parsley and bay leaves that was awarded to the victor in athletic competition.

10 Exhortations—Philippians 4:2-9

THREE-PART AGENDA

ICE-BREAKER	BIBLE STUDY	CARING TIME
15 Minutes	30 Minutes	15–45 Minutes

 LEADER: Has your group discussed its plans on what to study after this course is finished? What about the mission project described on page M6 in the center section?

TO BEGIN THE BIBLE STUDY TIME
(Choose 1 or 2)

1. Growing up, who in your family were you most likely to disagree with?

2. Who is the peacemaker in your family now? How does he or she do it?

3. What stresses you out: A trip to the dentist? A job interview? A parent / teacher conference?

READ SCRIPTURE & DISCUSS
(If you don't have time for all the questions in this section, coclude the Bible Study [30 min.] by answering question #8.)

1. When it comes to handling a conflict with another, are you more likely to confront or avoid that person? How do you feel about the way you handle conflict?

2. How does Paul advise the Philippians to deal with conflict and disagreement?

3. How often do you feel like rejoicing: Always? Almost always? Sometimes? Almost never? Only on special occasions and when the sun is shining?

Exhortations

²*I plead with Euodia and I plead with Syntyche to agree with each other in the Lord. ³Yes, and I ask you, loyal yoke-fellow,ᵃ help these women who have contended at my side in the cause of the gospel, along with Clement and the rest of my fellow workers, whose names are in the book of life.*

⁴*Rejoice in the Lord always. I will say it again: Rejoice! ⁵Let your gentleness be evident to all. The Lord is near. ⁶Do not be anxious about anything, but in everything, by prayer and petition, with thanksgiving, present your requests to God. ⁷And the peace of God, which transcends all understanding, will guard your hearts and your minds in Christ Jesus.*

⁸*Finally, brothers, whatever is true, whatever is noble, whatever is right, whatever is pure, whatever is lovely, whatever is admirable—if anything is excellent or praiseworthy—think about such things. ⁹Whatever you have learned or received or heard from me, or seen in me—put it into practice. And the God of peace will be with you.*

ᵃ3 Or *loyal Syzygus*

4. On a scale from 1 (low) to 10 (high), what is the stress level in your life right now?

5. What do you do to relieve stress from worry in your life? What does Paul say to do?

6. How does what you think about affect how you feel? How does it affect your relationship to God?

7. Looking at verse 8, what are some things you can think about that fit these characteristics?

8. Where do you need God's peace in your life right now?

CARING TIME
(Choose 1 or 2 of these questions before taking prayer requests and closing in prayer.)

1. Next week will be your last session in this study. How would you like to celebrate: A dinner? A party?

2. If your group plans to continue, what would you like to study next (see inside the back cover for what's available from Serendipity)?

3. How can the group pray for you this week?

Summary. Paul now pinpoints the specific problem confronting the Philippian church. Two of its leaders—Euodia and Syntyche—have had a falling out. And their disunity is threatening the unity of the whole church. (It is easy to imagine individuals lining up behind one or the other of these women so that factions develop.) In this unit, Paul first identifies the source of the disunity and urges resolution of the problem. But he does not stop at that point. Then he launches into a series of admonitions, which if followed, will enable them to "stand firm in the Lord" (4:1). He identifies those attitudes which enable people to cope successfully in difficult times.

4:2 plead. This is a strong verb, meaning "to exhort, to implore, to beg." The issue is so serious that Paul is willing to go on bended knee, as it were, to get it resolved. Paul uses this verb twice in verse 2 in order to underline the earnestness of his appeal. He also uses it twice to make it very clear that he is speaking to both of the contending parties. It is not a matter of one of them being in the wrong (and thus obliged to mend the split) while the other is in the right (and therefore without responsibility to work this out). Resolution will take work on the part of both women.

Euodia / Syntyche. Unlike most Greek women who remained in the background and had little to do with public life, Macedonian women were in every way as active and involved as the men. A businesswoman, Lydia, was Paul's first convert in Philippi. She organized the first house church there. These two women are, apparently, leaders in the Philippian church. Their opinions are very important, so much so that their quarrel is threatening to split the church. Their unity is crucial to the unity of the whole body.

in the Lord. The only hope for this kind of unity to develop between these two women is found in the fact of their common commitment to Jesus. To be "in the Lord" is to emulate the mindset of the Lord. As Paul has already pointed out, this means that they are to forsake self-serving attitudes and instead embrace the self-giving attitude that the Lord demonstrated in his incarnation (2:1–11).

4:3 loyal yokefellow. There has been much speculation about the identity of the person addressed here by Paul. He may simply be an unnamed colleague of Paul. Hawthorne feels that it is the whole church which is being called upon to help these women. Some suggest that the Greek word used here could be translated as if it were a proper name, *Syzygus*, in which case Paul would be reminding him to be true to his name ("loyal yokefellow") by assisting these women to resolve their differences.

fellow workers. These women are numbered among the company of those (like Clement and "the rest") who have struggled side by side with Paul in the hard work of spreading the Gospel. There is no hint—as some of the earlier commentators suggested—that Euodia and Syntyche merely worked among other women, or had a lesser role in ministry.

4:4 Rejoice. Paul returns to this central admonition which pervades the whole epistle. This is the first of a series of attitudes that make it possible to cope successfully in a hard situation. If one is rejoicing, one cannot be despairing. Paul is not calling for people to rejoice because of the situation. Rather, it is the Lord who is the source and cause of rejoicing.

in the Lord. Faith in the Lord makes joyfulness both realistic and possible, despite persecution and trouble.

4:5 gentleness. Not only are the Philippians to rejoice, they are to display this attitude toward others. It is the attitude of "graciousness" or "magnanimity" which is shown in situations when one could stand on his or her "rights," and yet for the sake of the other, does not insist on these rights.

The Lord is near. It is possible to rejoice and to act with gentleness because the Lord will return in the very near future and bring to an end all one's trials and difficulties. The Lord is "near" in a second sense as well. He is close to his children, via his Spirit, aiding them as they face these difficulties.

4:6 Do not be anxious. They are to "stop worrying." This is not a command given lightly. The Philippians certainly had cause to worry, and Paul (who writes this command) is in prison. Yet to worry is to display a lack of confidence in God's care and in God's control over the situation (see Matt. 6:25–34).

prayer / petition / requests. Paul uses three synonyms in a row to describe the alternative to anxiety. Instead of worrying, a person ought to converse directly with God and lay out before him all that is on his or her mind, confident that God will hear and respond.

with thanksgiving. When one is able to pray "with thanksgiving," anxiety is dealt with.

4:7 the peace of God. This is the only time that this phrase is used in the New Testament. It is part of God's inner character, and also what he experiences. Amazingly, it is this peace which he offers to share with his children.

transcends all understanding. Such peace can never fully be understood by human beings. It is the kind of peace which can never be figured out or produced by people themselves. It is that peace which relieves anxiety in a way quite beyond what people can do on their own.

guard. This is a military term. It describes a garrison of soldiers, such as those stationed at Philippi, whose job it is to stand watch over the city and protect it.

4:8 Finally. This word signals the end of the commands which Paul gives to the Philippians.

whatever is. Paul lists a series of virtues—perhaps drawn from the teaching of the philosophers of his day (since these are unusual words not used in this sense elsewhere in Paul's writings). Paul encourages them to reflect critically on ("think about") that which is:

true—sincerity and accuracy not only in thought and word, but in deed and attitude.

noble—those majestic things which command respect and which lift up one's mind from the mundane.

right—literally, "just," giving to God and others that which is their due.

pure—in all spheres of life—ideas, actions, motives, etc.

lovely—a warmth that calls forth love from others.

admirable—what people think only good things about.

Think about that which is:

TRUE—sincerity and accuracy not only in thought and word, but in deed and attitude.

NOBLE—those majestic things which command respect and which lift up one's mind from the mundane.

RIGHT—"just," giving to God and others that which is their due.

PURE—in all spheres of life—ideas, actions, motives, etc.

LOVELY—a warmth that calls forth love from others.

ADMIRABLE—what people think only good things about.

EXCELLENT—moral excellence.

PRAISEWORTHY—behavior that is universally praised.

---

excellent—moral excellence.

praiseworthy—behavior that is universally praised.

In other words, Paul is urging the Philippians to practice the kind of morality and behavior that would be commended even by their pagan colleagues. It is not surprising that his list of virtues is not unique to Christianity but drawn from the best of pagan culture.

4:9 Yet there is a style of life which goes beyond pagan goodness. Ultimately their behavior ought to reflect the commandments of God, which will at times be different from what popular culture commends.

learned / received / heard / seen. Paul identifies four sources of these commands. They were learned from the teaching of Paul (and others in the church); from the revelation of God (in the Old Testament and in the teachings of Jesus); and by what they hear and see in Paul's life.

11 Thanks for the Gifts—Phil. 4:10–23

THREE-PART AGENDA

ICE-BREAKER
15 Minutes

BIBLE STUDY
30 Minutes

CARING TIME
15–45 Minutes

 LEADER: Check page M7 of the center section for a good ice-breaker for this last session.

TO BEGIN THE BIBLE STUDY TIME
(Choose 1 or 2)

1. How's the weather in your life right now: Sunny? Partly cloudy? Stormy?

2. What was a particularly happy time in your life?

3. What is the best gift you have ever received?

READ SCRIPTURE & DISCUSS
(If you don't have time for all the questions in this section, conclude the Bible Study [30 min.] by answering question #7.)

1. How "content" are you right now? What outside force or circumstance is most likely to upset your contentment?

2. What is Paul's secret to contentment (vv. 10–13)? How does Paul's view of contentment compare with the modern world's view of contentment?

3. If Paul has learned to get along without, why does he commend the church in Philippi for sending a gift (vv. 14–17)?

4. How can Paul's attitude toward giving and receiving enable you to be a better giver? How can it enable you to be a better receiver?

Thanks for Their Gifts

10I rejoice greatly in the Lord that at last you have renewed your concern for me. Indeed, you have been concerned, but you had no opportunity to show it. 11I am not saying this because I am in need, for I have learned to be content whatever the circumstances. 12I know what it is to be in need, and I know what it is to have plenty. I have learned the secret of being content in any and every situation, whether well fed or hungry, whether living in plenty or in want. 13I can do everything through him who gives me strength.

14Yet it was good of you to share in my troubles. 15Moreover, as you Philippians know, in the early days of your acquaintance with the gospel, when I set out from Macedonia, not one church shared with me in the matter of giving and receiving, except you only; 16for even when I was in Thessalonica, you sent me aid again and again when I was in need. 17Not that I am looking for a gift, but I am looking for what may be credited to your account. 18I have received full payment and even more; I am amply supplied, now that I have received from Epaphroditus the gifts you sent. They are a fragrant offering, an acceptable sacrifice, pleasing to God. 19And my God will meet all your needs according to his glorious riches in Christ Jesus.

20To our God and Father be glory for ever and ever. Amen.

Final Greetings

21Greet all the saints in Christ Jesus. The brothers who are with me send greetings. 22All the saints send you greetings, especially those who belong to Caesar's household.

*23The grace of the Lord Jesus Christ be with your spirit. Amen.*a

---

a23 Some manuscripts do not have *Amen.*

5. What situations in your life are you feeling insecure about? How can verses 13 and 19 help you?

6. What has been the most valuable thing you've learned from studying Philippians?

7. What need do you have right now that you would like God to meet?

CARING TIME
(Choose 1 or 2 of these questions before taking prayer requests and closing in prayer.)

1. What was the "serendipity" in your group experience—the unexpected blessing?

2. Have you decided on three people in your group who are going to be commissioned to start a new group in the future?

3. How would you like the group to continue praying for you?

Summary. Paul has completed the body of his letter. He has said all that needs to be said. What remains now is for him to finish off his letter with a few "housekeeping" comments. Specifically, he thanks the Philippians for their gift—albeit in a rather curious fashion (vv. 10–20)—and then he passes along greetings from various people (vv. 21–23).

The way that Paul concludes his letter to the Philippians (vv. 10–23) is similar to the way in which most New Testament letters are concluded. As Houlden points out, typically there are four elements in this pattern. These are: (a) personal information and instructions (vv. 10–19); (b) a formal benediction or doxology (v. 20); (c) a brief, personal and less formal request (vv. 21–22); and (d) a final, simple benediction (v. 23). This structure fits the two-fold purpose of most New Testament letters. They were both general communications to whole churches as well as personal letters to friends. Thus, elements (a) and (b) concern the public part of the letter while elements (c) and (d) are addressed to friends.

4:10–19 It is difficult for Paul to know how to thank the Philippians properly for the gift which they sent him via Epaphroditus. The problem is this. While he affirmed the right of an apostle to be supported by the church, he personally refused to accept such gifts, preferring to underwrite his own ministry by working as a tentmaker (Acts 18:3; 1 Thess. 2:5–12; 2 Thess. 3:7–12). As he explains elsewhere (1 Cor. 9:1–23), he did this so that no one could ever accuse him of preaching the Gospel in order to make money, or say that the Gospel was anything but a free gift from God. But the Philippians have sent him a gift—and this is not the first time. And while he is genuinely grateful, he also wants to assert his independence. So, his problem is how to thank them while simultaneously asking them not to send any more money. In these verses, he manages this difficult balancing act with grace and skill.

4:10 I rejoice greatly in the Lord. This is the closest Paul gets to saying "thank you" to the Philippians. In this section about thanks, he does not once use the word "thanks"! Still, this is not an insincere expression on Paul's part. In fact, he says that he "rejoices greatly" over what they have done. This is the only time in his letters that Paul ever adds a qualifier to "rejoicing," thus emphasizing the depth of his feelings toward the Philippians.

that ... you have been concerned. The cause of his rejoicing is not the gift, per se, but the concern that it evidenced.

> *To be a Christian is not merely a matter of creedal confession, church membership, rule keeping, or ritual practice. To be a Christian is to be "in Christ Jesus." It is this reality that makes all the difference.*

at last. Apparently, the Philippians had not been in contact with Paul for quite some time. The reason for this is not explained. However, the arrival of Epaphroditus renewed their contact with Paul for which he is grateful.

renewed. This is a rare Greek word which appears only at this place in the New Testament. It describes the flowering of a bush or tree and can be translated "blossomed." Paul is so grateful for their renewed care after this long silence that to him it is like seeing a shoot sprout out of the ground and burst into blossom.

Indeed, you have been concerned. Paul is not criticizing them for not being in touch. It is not that they did not want to come to his aid. They simply had no opportunity.

4:11 Having expressed his pleasure at this sign of their care, he goes on to say: "But, in fact, I really did not need what you gave me!" This is the first of several alternations between commending them for their gift (vv. 10,14–16,18–20) and insisting on his right to self-sufficiency (vv. 11–13,17).

need. This is another rare word, used only here and in Mark 12:44. It means "poverty" or "lack." Paul was not in difficult straits financially. He accepts their gift only because it is of great benefit to them to give in this way (see vv. 17–18).

content. Another rare word. This is its only appearance in the New Testament. Paul borrows it from the vocabulary of the Stoic philosophers, for whom it was a favorite word. It was used to describe the person who was self-sufficient and able to exist without anything or anyone. Paul's sufficiency is found in the Lord.

4:12 need. This is a different Greek word from the one translated "need" in verse 11. This word refers to the lowering of water in a river. As such, it is a reference to fundamental needs which are basic to life (such as food and water). Paul has learned to exist even in the midst of abject poverty.

plenty. This is the opposite state of "need." It means literally, "to overflow," that is, to have enough for one's own daily needs plus something left over. In Luke 9:17 it refers to the food left over after Jesus fed the 5,000. Although the root idea is not that of opulent luxury, the word came to mean extreme riches. In this verse, Paul is contrasting two extremes: deprivation (when one lacks even the basic necessities of life), and riches (when one has far more than what one could possibly use).

I have learned the secret. This is the only occurrence of this verb in the New Testament. It is drawn from the world of the mystery religions and refers to the rites by which the initiate comes to understand the secret of the cult.

well fed. This is a word which describes force-fed animals who are stuffed to overflowing in order to fatten them for slaughter. It is used by Paul to define one of the extremes: having more than enough to eat.

hungry. This is the opposite condition. It refers to the absence of food.

living in plenty or want. Another set of contrasting words. It is by the experience of these extremes that Paul has come to know the secret of coping with all circumstances.

4:13 everything. A better translation of this word would be "all these things." Paul is referring to what he has just described: his ability to exist in all types of material circumstances—wealth or poverty, abundant food or no food, etc. He is not suddenly making a general statement about his ability to do anything.

> *While it is true that by going through a variety of difficult circumstances Paul has learned the discipline necessary to cope with hardship and abundance, it is also true that this ability is not merely self-generated. It comes from Christ.*

through him who gives me strength. The source of Paul's ability to exist successfully in all circumstances is his union with Christ. This is his "secret." While it is true that by going through a variety of difficult circumstances he has learned the discipline necessary to cope with hardship and abundance, it is also true that this ability is not merely self-generated. It comes from Christ. This is an illustration on an individual level of 2:12–13. Paul is working out his own salvation ("health," "wholeness") while at the same time, God is working in him (see also 2 Cor. 12: 9–10).

4:14 Paul shifts from the issue of his self-sufficiency back to their act of generosity. They did a really beautiful thing by becoming partners in his hardships.

4:16 again and again. This is one of the few churches from which Paul has accepted multiple gifts—which is an indicator of the special relationship he has with the Philippians.

4:17 Not that I am looking. Paul flips back to the other side of the question: his independence.

4:18 even more / amply supplied. Paul is pleading with them not to send further gifts.

a fragrant offering, an acceptable sacrifice. Paul now shifts his metaphor from the world of banking to the world of religion, specifically, to the idea of a sacrificial system. The gift to Paul was also a gift to God, similar to the sweet odor of animal sacrifice offered up to God.

4:21 all the saints. This is the private portion of his letter and yet Paul does not ask that his special greetings be addressed only to particular individuals whom he names. Instead, he asks that each person in the Philippian church be greeted. In this way, Paul

Notes—(cont.)

emphasizes once again that he is not taking sides in whatever dispute is going on. They are all his friends and he wants each of them to be greeted personally on his behalf.

in Christ Jesus. For one final time Paul uses this phrase. It is, of course, one of his favorite phrases. He uses it literally hundreds of times in his letters. By it he describes the essence of what it means to be a Christian. To be a Christian is not merely a matter of creedal confession, church membership, rule keeping, or ritual practice. To be a Christian is to be "in Christ Jesus." It is this reality that makes all the difference.

The brothers. It is not just Paul, but the ministry team he is a part of, that send greetings. Who these "brothers" are is not specified, but certainly they would include people like Timothy. This is not a reference to the church at Rome since it is mentioned in the next sentence.

4:22 *All the saints.* The Christians in Rome are the third group that sends greetings.

Caesar's household. From among the church as a whole, a particular group wishes to make known its greetings, namely those who serve on the imperial staff. This is not a reference to the actual family of Caesar. Rather, it denotes those of both high and low rank who are involved in the running of the empire. This includes, soldiers, administrators, servants, high officials, etc. They are eager to meet the folk in Philippia because it is a Roman colony. Paul's use of the phrase "Caesar's household" is significant. It is an indication that Christianity had now begun to penetrate the government of the Roman Empire.

> *The source of Paul's ability to exist successfully in all circumstances is his union with Christ. This is his "secret."*

4:23 *grace.* Paul began this letter by pronouncing "grace and peace" upon the Philippians (1:2). He ends on the same note—but with an interesting twist. At the beginning of the letter he spoke about grace "from God our Father and the Lord Jesus Christ." Here it is simply "the grace of the Lord Jesus Christ." In Paul's mind, Christ is the fit and full mediator of the grace of God. It is his grace since he partakes of the divine nature.

your spirit. "Your" is plural and "spirit" is singular. What Paul prays is that the grace of Christ will rest on each individual believer in Philippi. The word "spirit" in this context is used to refer to the whole person, especially in his or her mental and spiritual aspects.

Acknowledgments

In preparing these notes, generous use was made of the traditional tools of New Testament research: *A Greek-English Lexicon of the New Testament* by Arndt & Gingrich; *New International Dictionary of New Testament Theology,* edited by Colin Brown; *The NIV Complete Concordance;* various New Testament "Introductions," etc. In addition, use was made of a variety of commentaries. While it is not possible, given the scope and aim of this book, to acknowledge in detail the influence of each author, the sources of direct quotes and special insights are noted. The key commentary used in the preparation of these notes is *Philippians* by Gerald F. Hawthorne (Word Biblical Commentary, Volume 43), Waco, TX: Word Books, 1983. This commentary had not been published when the first draft of these notes was written in 1981. However, it aided greatly in the expansion and revision of the materials in 1985. Other commentaries frequently consulted include: *Philippians* by Ralph P. Martin (The New Century Bible Commentary), Grand Rapids, MI: Wm. B. Eerdmans Publishing Co., 1976; *Philippians* by F. F. Bruce (A Good News Commentary), San Francisco: Harper & Row, 1983; *A Translators Handbook on Paul's Letter to the Philippians* by I-Jin Loh Loh and Eugene A. Nida (Helps for Translators), United Bible Societies, 1977; and *The Letters to the Philippians, Colossians and Thessalonians* by William Barclay (The Daily Study Bible), Edinburgh: The Saint Andrew Press, 1959.

Reference was also made to *Paul's Letters from Prison: Philippians, Colossians, Philemon and Ephesians* by J. L. Houlden (Westminster Pelican Commentaries), Philadelphia: The Westminster Press, 1970, 1977; *A Critical and Exegetical Commentary on the Epistles to the Philippians and to Philemon* by Marvin R. Vincent (The International Critical Commentary) Edinburgh: T. & T. Clark, 1987; *The Message of Philippians: Jesus our Joy,* by Alec Motyer (The Bible Speaks Today), Downers Grove, IL: InterVarsity Press, 1984; *Philippians: Jesus our Joy* by Donald Baker (A Lifebuilder Bible Study) Downers Grove, IL: InterVarsity Press, 1985; *The Epistles of Paul to the Philippians and to Philemon* by J. J. Muller (The New International Commentary on the New Testament) Grand Rapids, MI: Wm. B. Eerdmans Publishing Co., 1955, 1980; and *Philippians and Colossians: Letters from Prison* by Marilyn Kunz and Catherine Schell (Neighborhood Bible Studies), Wheaton, IL: Tyndale House Publishers, 1972.

Caring Time Notes